From Cogs to Code

A Blueprint for Future-Proofing Your Career in the Automation Age

Alexander Hastings

Table of Contents

Chapter 1: The Evolution of Work

Over time, how we work has changed a lot. First, big factories with machines took over, making things like textiles and steel. This made cities grow fast and changed how society worked. Then, in the 1900s, we entered the Information Age. This is when computers and the internet became important. People started doing less manual labor and more work with data, like using computers to organize information. The way we think about work has also changed because of this. Technology keeps changing quickly, and it affects almost every job. Some jobs will disappear because machines can do them, but new jobs will come up, too. People will need to learn new skills to keep up with these changes. As technology advances, adapting to new skills and ways of working will be crucial for navigating the evolving landscape of employment in the information age.

Automation and Its Historical Context

Automation has become one of the fundamental elements in human history. To fully grasp the importance of automation, we must embark on a historical trip that explores its origins, tracing back to where mechanization first started.

The story starts in the late eighteenth century—a period when the Industrial Revolution laid its roots. The first efforts at automation were made with the introduction of water- and steam-powered machinery, which redefined manual production methods. The textile industry facilitated these changes thanks to innovations such as spinning yarn and power looms. These inventions improved efficiency and paved the way for industrial mechanization.

Fast forward to the nineteenth century, and new inventions like the steam engine changed everything. Trains and steamships made transportation faster, which led to significant changes in how things were made. Factories got bigger and used more machines, changing how people worked. Instead of handcrafting items, machines started doing more work, transforming the labor scene.

In the twentieth century, many new inventions made work easier and faster. One example is Henry Ford's assembly line, which made producing things quickly and in large quantities possible. This changed how industries worked and the types of jobs available. People started using electricity more, which helped automate repetitive tasks. It set the stage for the digital age we're in now.

Computers and programmable logic controllers emerged in the latter half of the twentieth century to revolutionize automation. In turn, technological innovations— computer numerical control (CNC), machine maturation, the emergence of robotics, and the appearance of artificial intelligence (AI)—pushed automation beyond limits. For example, CNC machining revolutionized precision engineering, while industrial robots took over complex and delicate tasks, leading the way in automation.

Because devices are now connected and software has become more powerful, a new wave of automation has transformed manufacturing and service industries. The rise of the internet and innovative technologies have further blurred the lines between physical and virtual automation. (Noble, 2017).

Technological Revolutions and Job Transformations

Automation isn't only about improving machines; it's also changed how people find jobs. This chapter discusses the sophisticated dance between technological revolutions and job transformation and how each wave of innovation transforms the workforce into a fluid environment that changes professional personas.

The Industrial Revolution marked a leap between labor and nature in the early nineteenth century. The automation of manual labor resulted in the emergence of large factories with a huge demand for industrial workers. But the boom in job vacancies was accompanied by a tectonic shift in the skills needed. As craftsmanship gradually ceased, the assembly line needed a new breed of workers skilled in carrying out repetitive, dull tasks.

In the second half of the twentieth century, a revolution

occurred due to the emergence of computers. They enhanced productivity and enabled new horizons of creativity, but they also set about a revolutionary change in jobs. Routine activities, especially in the manufacturing and clerical sectors, were computerized, leading to the loss of some jobs. In contrast, others presented new job opportunities for those well-versed in emerging technology.

Eventually, another turning point was the digital revolution of the late twentieth and early twenty-first centuries. Computers and the internet became ubiquitous, transforming entire industries. From the emergence of eCommerce to AI and machine learning, employment has wholly changed. The need for software developers, data analysts, and cyber security experts rose rapidly as traditional jobs were facing obsolescence. This period changed job specifications and prompted the emergence of entirely new professions that were unthinkable just a few years ago.

The formation and decline of positions have become an essential feature of all revolutionary shifts. The World Economic Forum's research indicates that in 2025, more than half of all jobs will be done by machines. Although this may bring along the age of efficiency, it is a dramatic change in what one means by work.

The fourth Industrial Revolution witnessed the renaissance of the manufacturing sector, which suffered significant job losses during industrialization. Factories have become intelligent, networked systems through automation, and the demand for jobs such as robotics technician or automation engineer has increased. Yet, the jobs on a traditional assembly line have been disappearing, which shows why reskilling and upskilling programs are so important (Herrmann et al., 2018).

In the field of services, AI and machine learning have fostered positions such as artificial intelligence experts, data scientists, or algorithm makers. At the same time, monotonous, routine job positions in customer service or data entry have declined. This is the ecosystem where adaptability to change becomes a critical skill, along with IT experts and digital communication specialists, due to increasing remote work, which was also accelerated by digitization.

As we traverse these statistics and witness the tide of new jobs and obsolescence, it becomes apparent that future work is not a stationary destination but an evolving pathway. Embracing changes, new skill acquisition, and adaptability reflect essential approaches suitable for facilitating the waves of job transformations brought by technological revolutions.

The Role of Education in Shaping Future Skills

Traditionally, education is the furnace in which skills are forged and knowledge shared so that individuals can always be ready to face the challenges of their careers. Nevertheless, education must reinvent itself in the digital era. Gone are the days when one's studies could meet all their life needs; education must become a self-development process that changes with technological development.

The changing status quo of education transcends the boundaries set by brick-and-mortar classrooms. Not limited to geographical boundaries, online learning platforms such as Massive Open Online Courses (MOOCs) and other digital resources have democratized access to the knowledge through which individuals can upskill or reskill. The focus is moving from blind memory to developing critical reasoning, ingenuity, and agility—factors that play a role in success when many industries become dependent on automation and AI mechanisms.

Besides, the partnership between educational bodies and industries becomes very necessary. Hence, ensuring that the curricula are updated to meet the changing requirements of the job market means that graduates know what they ought to know and the practical skills employers need. The difference between academic knowledge and practical implementation is bridged by internships, apprenticeships, and experiential learning opportunities, ensuring a smooth transition from academics to the work environment.

As the workplace landscape evolves, so does the need for versatile skills. Adaptive skills include a range of attributes, from innovative and analytic thinking to empathy and IT prowess. Such skills withstand automation and allow people to succeed in volatile, ambiguous contexts.

Adaptability, in this sense, means a lot more than just learning new technologies. It includes the ability to change careers, a willingness to accept changes with a growth mindset, and constantly evaluating and refining one's skills. The World Economic Forum's report shows that problem-solving, self-management, and emotional intelligence will be among the most demanded skills sought by employers in 2025, suggesting that adaptability is no longer a nice thing to have but an absolute necessity for success.

Thus, education must be a big stimulus for developing such adaptive abilities. It must develop a passion for learning, increase curiosity, and serve as the basis on which self-improvement is built. The entities that understand the need for adaptability will influence us as we mold the individuals who are survivors and thrivers in this age of automation (Whiteman, 2023).

Conclusion

Our journey through this chapter has served two purposes. It's been a look back at the past and a guide to help us navigate the challenges we face in our careers. Education plays a crucial role in this journey, adapting to the times in and out of the classroom. We always need to be ready to learn and improve throughout our lives.

As we reflect on our journey in Chapter 1, one big lesson stands out: The future of work isn't just a distant idea; it's happening right now. It's a dynamic and fair system that rewards hard work and creativity. The Evolution of Work is like a seed planted today, with the potential to grow into something extraordinary.

So, let's keep talking about the lessons from history and how they relate to technology and skills. Our journey continues, and each new chapter helps us prepare for the future in the Automation Age. Let's celebrate our progress, acknowledge our setbacks, and keep pushing forward. These ideas will guide us as we move into a future where change is constant, but progress never stops.

Chapter 2: The Rise of Automation

Automation is drastically changing how industries operate, making them more efficient by utilizing machines, calculators, and robotics in the workforce. Such complex tasks no longer perplex these technologies; for instance, robots in manufacturing and automated customer services can be found everywhere. Algorithms in finance and healthcare use data to inform decision-making and provide services with a higher standard, and robotics manage repetitive or complex sections.

Implementing new ideas within a company can yield both positive and negative outcomes. While changes may seem progressive initially, they can also pose challenges. Workers may need to acquire new skills, embrace adaptable thinking, and foster innovative approaches to adapt to these changes. This process can be particularly daunting with the introduction of technologies like automation. While automation offers benefits, it can also disrupt communities. Consequently, companies must strike a balance between adopting new technology and preparing individuals for the future. Embracing emerging technologies such as AI and blockchain presents companies with diverse challenges, as they swiftly transform society and the economy.

Automation Technologies Overview

Artificial Intelligence (AI)

AI is a sub-branch of computer science that seeks to develop intelligent machines and systems designed to function like human beings, process cognitive data, and perform tasks carried out by humans with much effort called skills (Verdegem, 2021). Different fields and technologies fall under it, all of which contribute to the development of making machines intelligent (Chan et al., 2022).

Machine Learning: Machine learning is one of the main aspects of artificial intelligence. It includes the creation of learning mechanisms and solutions that allow machines to teach themselves based on data for optimization with no direct encoding; in other words, model-based machine learning. Machine learning algorithms analyze large volumes of data, identify patterns within the data, and use this information to make predictions or decisions.

Natural Language Processing (NLP): NLP is a branch of artificial intelligence that deals with research that makes machines interpret, comprehend, and generate language. It enables humans to exchange data with computers through speaking or text formats.

AI can be used in many applications, such as:

Optimal Decision-Making: The concept of decision-making has been revolutionized by AI in our corporate world. Such businesses can also use AI algorithms to automate complicated processes such as data analysis or perform simple operations that would have otherwise required a human hand—this improvement in practice results in better and more precise decision-making.

Personalization: AI helps interact face-to-face, according to a person's expectations of the product or service and attributes. AI-assisted recommendation systems grade user behavior and preferences to make recommendations based on consumer demand, delivered through personalized content such as movies, product offers, or user encounters. This personalization improves customer satisfaction, which translates into higher levels of engagement.

Medicine and Health Care: AI is critical in the medical field since it helps detect diseases, mainly those challenging to diagnose without laboratory equipment, and forms treatment plans. Machine learning models can identify anomalies through medical images such as X-rays and MRIs, which help healthcare personnel provide accurate diagnoses. Besides, AI-based chatbots and virtual health assistants also support healthcare information meant to be sent through a coordinated case management system and shown on an operating room display screen.

Research and Development: In the process of research and development, AI has a way that enables the acceleration of discovery rates. AI uses algorithms that process data at exceptional levels and identify patterns in massive datasets, which would never be feasible for an ordinary human to do manually. This assists in genomics, material science, and drug discovery for researchers.

Automation: AI is significantly impacting various industries by automating tasks. Robotic Process Automation (RPA) aims to decrease the need for human workers in specific tasks and reduce errors. Its main goal is to free up business space for people to take on more creative and strategic roles. AI-powered automation is improving efficiency in sectors like manufacturing and logistics.

Autonomous Vehicles: Self-driving cars, or autonomous vehicles, rely on AI technology to operate in self-drive mode. These vehicles use sensors, cameras, and AI algorithms to navigate while driving. The emergence of autonomous vehicles represents a new technological frontier that will transform our transportation system. They promise to revolutionize how we get around by reducing accidents and optimizing travel time.

Customer Service and Chatbots: Most AI-driven chatbots and virtual assistants permeate the industry as they work round the clock to handle queries and address user needs. They improve customer care by sending frequent answers and minimizing response time.

Finance and Trading: The use of AI in the finance industry is widely prevalent, with algorithmic trading fraud detection, credit scoring, and risk assessment being the most common. With AI, models analyze financial data quickly and accurately, enabling fast fraud-resistant trading decisions.

Robotics

The joining of automation and robotics is like a technological curve that has made integration one major junction for robots (Mckinnon, 2015).

Manufacturing: Robots are being used in various tasks that require precision, such as assembly, welding, painting, and quality checks. They work tirelessly and consistently, leading to improved production with fewer mistakes. Collaborative robots, or cobots, enhance safety and productivity by working alongside humans in manufacturing operations.

Logistics and Warehousing: Automated Guided Vehicles (AGVs) and Autonomous Mobile Robots (AMRs) are innovative mobile logistics solutions used in warehouses. They handle material handling tasks autonomously. Semi-automation practices are implemented in warehouse operations where material handling is required.

Robots using AI and computer vision technologies can help employees navigate warehouses and identify items in storage units to ensure proper inventory management.

Healthcare and Surgery: Robots in healthcare have undergone a major revolutionary transformation by maneuvering surgeons to practice surgery with minimal invasions. The robotic surgical systems are bringing a lot of accuracy, and by reducing the invasiveness, post-surgery recovery is getting faster.

Telemedicine robots create a virtual doctor-patient communication environment, bringing access to medical resources and referrals to remote areas.

Agriculture: Technological advancements in agriculture have led to research in drones and autonomous tractors, changing how farmers do their business. They can plant seeds, care for the plants' health issues, and carry out things such as weeding during crop growth stages while harvesting when they grow.

Precision agriculture provided by robotics and automation aims to use resources effectively in terms of cost regarding the crop yields produced.

Autonomous Robots: A combination of AI interwoven with robotics has resulted in independent robots that can make profound decisions and respond flexibly.

Self-driving cars, delivery robots, and any devices or systems designed to operate independently without human intervention are examples of autonomous robotic embodiments.

Space Exploration and Exploration: Robots play an essential role in space exploration. Remotely controlled robots, such as Curiosity and Perseverance, drive missions to Mars' surface, destinations for robotic explorers.

Earth-based platforms that require human beings in autonomous drones and submarines often explore harsh, remote environments, such as deep-sea explorations or emergencies.

Household and Personal Use: In households, people utilize robotic vacuum cleaners, popular garden mowers, and many other companions that help in their day-to-day activities, such as social robotics.

Such robots reduce routine everyday activities, enrich through the provision of entertainment, and also bring companionship.

Internet of Things (IoT)

The Internet of Things (IoT) is a network that connects physical objects, like appliances or devices, with sensors and software to share data. This connection allows for automation and intelligent decision-making in various areas that were once beyond the reach of technology. For example, smart homes can adjust temperature and lighting based on occupants' preferences, while intelligent cities can manage traffic flow efficiently and conserve energy. IoT enables real-time monitoring and maintenance of equipment in industries, reducing downtime and increasing efficiency. The data collected by IoT devices feeds into AI systems, creating a cycle of optimization and innovation (Greengard, 2015).

The Impact of AI, Robotics, and IoT

Industry Impact

Manufacturing Revolution: It all began with the arrival of robotics and IoT in manufacturing, commonly known as Industry 4.0, which has changed production lines completely. Production efficiency and safety have increased tremendously as robots take over repetitive, dangerous, and precise tasks. IoT devices allow for real-time machine monitoring and predictive maintenance, which reduces downtime and prolongs the life cycle of equipment.

Healthcare Transformation: AI is transforming medicine in a big way. AI algorithms make medical services more accurate and efficient, from diagnosing illnesses to creating personalized treatment plans. Robotic endoscopy provides ultra-precise procedures that even surpass what human surgeons can do. Meanwhile, IoT devices ensure patients are continuously monitored, leading to better patient outcomes and helping healthcare providers deliver better care.

Agriculture Modernization: Powered by this technology, precision agriculture enables more intelligent decision-making in farming. Robotics in the form of drones, AI-driven soil, and crop health analytics that are IoT-driven for real-time data from field conditions all together go into providing higher yields with environmentally friendly farming practices.

Retail and Supply Chain Innovation: In retail, AI-powered predictive analytics are changing inventory management and customer service, while robotics in warehousing and logistics are cutting down on mistakes and making supply chains more efficient. IoT devices allow for real-time tracking, ensuring transparency and efficiency in managing the supply chain.

Economic Impact

Productivity Growth: Automation has revolutionized productivity by simplifying procedures, eliminating human errors, and hastening production. This has increased output rates and cost savings on operations, positively leading to economies' GDP.

Job Market Transformation: These technologies have replaced many manual and repetitive jobs, but they have also brought in new job categories requiring AI, robotics, and IoT maintenance skills. This dynamic shift requires workforce reskilling and upskilling, which points out the role of adaptation in the labor market.

Business Model Innovation: Since the introduction of these technologies, many new business models have emerged. Organizations provide products as a service based on IoT for product tracking and AI, as well as service personalization, allowing new ways to generate revenue and customer engagement strategies.

Global Competition and Inequality: Uneven adoption and access to advanced technologies have created disparities among countries and companies, impacting international competitiveness. Nations and corporations leveraging these technologies gain a significant competitive advantage, leaving others lagging.

The Ethical Dilemmas of Automation

The rapid growth of AI, robotics, and IoT technologies has changed industries and economies and raised various ethical concerns. These include biases in AI systems, job losses due to automation, and privacy issues. It's crucial to address these concerns to ensure that the benefits of automation are distributed fairly and equitably in society.

1. Biases in AI Systems

AI intelligence systems are unbiased and based only on the data they were trained with. Historical data may frequently perpetuate the existing biases that result in discriminatory AI systems based on race, gender, and more.

Statistical Perspective: The study conducted by the Massachusetts Institute of Technology (MIT) Media Lab (2018) (Hardesty, 2018) showed that the facial recognition technologies of big tech firms had 5.4 times higher error rates concerning dark-skinned females than white men, which stood at only 3%. This gap highlights the intrinsic bias in AI systems.

Addressing the Issue: To ensure ethical AI, it's important to actively work on making training datasets diverse and inclusive. Testing should be done from various demographic perspectives to ensure fairness. Transparency in AI algorithms and decision-making processes can help identify and address biases.

2. Job Displacement Issues

The rise of automation technologies has created challenges, such as job loss, despite efficiency and productivity gains. The concern extends beyond just losing jobs to the rapid changes in the skills needed for new roles created by automation.

Statistical Perspective: According to a report by the World Economic Forum (2020), automation and restructuring work between humans and machines were expected to displace around 85 million jobs globally by 2026. However, the report also predicted creating approximately 97 million new jobs. This suggests a complex shift in the labor market rather than simply reducing employment.

Addressing the Issue: It's crucial to prioritize reskilling and upskilling efforts to prepare the workforce for the future. Governments, educational institutions, and industries should collaborate to provide training programs and make education responsive to the changing demands of the job market. Social safety nets and transitional programs are essential to support individuals affected by automation job displacement.

3. Privacy Concerns with IoT

The interrelatedness of IoT devices creates significant privacy concerns. If the information about individuals collected by IoT devices is not handled and protected well, there are many opportunities for privacy breaches.

Statistical Perspective: A survey conducted by The Economist Intelligence Unit in 2017 found that executives from various industries worldwide believe that 92% of the Internet of Things (IoT) will have significant privacy implications. One primary concern highlighted is data security.

Addressing the Issue: On the flip side, improving cybersecurity practices, enforcing strict data governance policies, and educating individuals about their privacy rights are essential steps in addressing privacy concerns. Regulations like the General Data Protection Regulation (GDPR) in Europe outline how personal data should be handled, requiring consent and providing protection.

Conclusion

As we navigate the transformative waves of AI, robotics, and IoT, industries, economies, and societies are experiencing profound changes. These technologies are not just tools for optimization and innovation but also shaping a new way of life for us all. Their impact is far-reaching, from revolutionizing manufacturing to changing how healthcare is delivered, from influencing consumer behavior to redefining urban spaces. They promise a future where advanced automation benefits everyone, not just the wealthy, driving growth and prosperity.

However, these promises come with challenges. Ethical concerns, such as biases in AI, job displacement, and privacy issues, remind us of the responsibility of using these powerful technologies. While statistics show significant progress and disruptions, they also highlight human innovation and adaptability. Despite projections of job loss due to automation, creating new opportunities suggests a transition rather than an end to the workforce. It's crucial for technological advancement to prioritize equity and fairness, as seen in disparities in error rates among different demographic groups in AI systems.

Chapter 3: Remote Work Revolution

Remote work has significantly changed today's workplace, primarily enabled by technology and events like the COVID-19 pandemic. Initially seen as a temporary solution, remote work has become a standard practice. Advancements in computer technology, cloud computing, collaborative online tools, virtual reality, and AI-driven platforms have made remote work not only possible but also more efficient. These technologies have improved accessibility and productivity, allowing people to work from anywhere easily.

This revolution goes beyond technology, reshaping corporate culture and the dynamics between leaders and employees. It requires addressing challenges like cybersecurity, maintaining group cohesion across various locations, and adapting to evolving work environments. This includes hybrid setups that combine remote and office formats.

Remote Work Trends and Statistics

Remote work has experienced rapid growth, surpassing expectations, from a significant milestone to becoming necessary for the global workforce (Sava, 2020). Fueled by technological advancements and global crises, this revolution has impacted businesses' work culture and operations worldwide. This segment explores the trends and statistics that paint a detailed picture of the remote work revolution, highlighting its evolution, influence, and driving factors.

Growth of Remote Work

Pre-Pandemic Baseline: Remote work was already rising before COVID-19 but has been primarily limited to specific sectors and job types. According to the Buffer 2019 report, around 30% of the workforce could work remotely. However, this was mostly a phenomenon in the technology space and among freelancers.

Pandemic-Driven Acceleration: The emergence of COVID-19 functions as a catalyst, which dramatically speeds up the process that was already ongoing. According to Gartner's (2020) report, after the advent of the COVID-19 crisis, more than 88% of companies across the globe required or persuaded their employees to work from home. This transformation was a short-term adaptation and the first step in a structural, institutional change in working patterns.

Post-Pandemic Trends: Virtual work remains popular as the world cautiously moves towards a post-pandemic reality. According to the Owl Labs survey conducted in 2021, 16% of companies worldwide are now fully remote, and more than half of employees work remotely, at least part-time.

Impact and Adoption Globally

Global Reach and Adoption: Remote work is widespread across different continents and is not limited to any particular location. While countries like the USA, the United Kingdom, and Australia are leading in adoption rates due to their solid technological infrastructure, developing countries are also catching up. They are leveraging mobile technology and the internet to bridge the gap and embrace remote work.

Sector-Specific Trends: Remote work has been adopted across various sectors and impacts different workforce levels. Thanks to the nature of their work, industries like IT and professional services have shown greater adaptability to remote working. However, manufacturing, healthcare, and retail sectors need more support due to their reliance on physical presence for operations.

Economic Implications: The economic impact of the remote work model is substantial. A recent Global Workplace Analytics (2020) study found that if half of employees with remote-compatible jobs worked from home, the United States could save $715 billion annually. These savings come from reduced expenses like real estate, utilities, absenteeism, and turnover rates.

Productivity and Performance

Productivity Insights: Remote work performance has often been positive despite initial skepticism. According to Prodoscore's 2021 report, productivity among remote workers increased by up to 47% during the year. Flexibility in scheduling work and reduced commute times have been crucial in this improvement.

Challenges and Adaptation: While productivity metrics are encouraging, remote work also presents difficulties in collaboration and communication and is set to reshape various domains entirely. However, companies are investing in improving collaborative technologies and fostering an environment of trust and flexibility to overcome these challenges.

Advantages and Disadvantages of Remote Work

The introduction of remote working has uncovered a complex mix of advantages and drawbacks, altering perspectives on productivity, work-life balance, and organizational culture. This section explores the nuanced benefits and inherent drawbacks of teleworking, offering a balanced perspective on this evolving work arrangement.

The Benefits

Flexibility and Work-Life Balance

Remote work flexibility doesn't just mean choosing when to work but rather a shift in how work is approached. This change enables employees to structure their workday around personal obligations, such as caring for family members or pursuing hobbies. This scheduling freedom is linked to improved mental health, reduced stress, and overall job satisfaction. Companies embracing this flexibility experience lower absenteeism and turnover rates.

However, organizations must cultivate a culture that respects boundaries, ensuring flexibility doesn't lead to an expectation of round-the-clock work.

Increased Productivity

Minimal noise distractions in remote work environments boost productivity by providing a focused working space without interruptions. However, this increased productivity relies on the right tools and resources. Investing in collaborative technologies, project management tools, and virtual meeting platforms can improve productivity. Regular feedback and open communication channels are essential for keeping remote teams on track and accountable.

Cost Savings

The benefits of remote work savings extend beyond the apparent savings from commuting or office expenses. For employers, reduced office space leads to significant savings on real estate rents, utility bills, and stationery—additionally, fewer corporate travel expenses and lower in-person meetings costs. Employees also save on clothing and home meals due to reduced commuting. These savings allow individuals to bolster their financial resources and allocate funds toward health, wellness, and career development.

The availability of a much broader talent pool is beneficial.

Telecommuting equalizes employment opportunities for everyone and eliminates regional boundaries, uncovering talents worldwide. This global influence enriches organizational culture with diverse perspectives and helps businesses find better solutions regardless of location. However, hiring from a worldwide talent pool presents challenges, as recruiting managers must navigate cultural differences, local employment regulations, and virtual onboarding.

Companies that effectively manage these complexities can build diverse and skilled teams.

Environmental Benefits

The impact of reduced commuting on the environment is significant. With fewer cars on the road, greenhouse gas emissions decrease, aiding the fight against climate change. Additionally, the need for larger office space results in a smaller ecological footprint in commercial real estate. However, it's essential to consider the overall impact of remote work on the environment and society, which also depends on the energy efficiency of home offices and the digital infrastructure supporting remote operations.

In essence, remote work's numerous benefits paint a promising labor future. However, realizing this potential requires intelligent strategies, robust infrastructure, and a supportive culture that balances flexibility with productivity and inclusivity. As the world embraces this new reality, both challenges and opportunities lie in our ability to create a working environment that is not only productive but also beneficial for all.

Challenges

Communication and Collaboration Challenges

The virtual barrier can hinder the accessible communication and collaboration that people often expect from a physical office environment. Miscommunications may occur. Without non-verbal expressions, misunderstandings can quickly arise.

Mitigation Strategies: Maintaining a connection through regular video meetings is possible. Collaborative tools like Slack, Microsoft Teams, or Asana help establish more transparent communication. Implementing a strict communication system and promoting an open-minded elicitation of ideas can result in stronger team relationships.

Overwork and Work-Life Boundaries

The very convenience of a home office may become one's curse, and the working hours can spill over into free time. This may result in burnout and decreased productivity as long-term consequences.

Mitigation Strategies: Companies can promote a healthy work-life balance by championing relaxing breaks and not infringing on off-hours. Working from home can be mentally separated by encouraging the employees to set up a proper workstation. By leading by example, managers highlight the essentiality of downtime.

Data Security Risks

Moving to home offices creates a new vulnerability because employees often use weak security measures on their home networks.

Mitigation Strategies: Data can be secured through solid security protocols, IT audits, and virtual private network (VPN) service provision. It is imperative to train the employees in the proper cybersecurity protocols. Companies need safe and trustworthy technology to keep their digital assets secure.

Performance Management and Oversight

In remote setups, the lack of physical supervision may cause many worries over employees' productivity rates and job completion.

Mitigation Strategies: Concentrate on the output and outcomes rather than micromanaging. Use project management tools to make the progress visible. Regular updates and defining goals that are objective and quantifiable can help employees and managers stay on the same page regarding their expectations and deliverables.

Inequality in Remote Work Accessibility

Not everyone can work remotely because some jobs require physical presence, and not everyone has the right environment at home for practical remote work.

Mitigation Strategies: Companies may offer allowances or provide resources for the workers to arrange a home office, ensuring that all employees have the right tools and settings. For non-remote roles, looking into flexible working hours or other benefits could help foster a more inclusive workplace culture.

Work-Life Balance

Maintaining work-life balance becomes crucial; it is not only about the well-being of the employees but also about productivity and having a healthy workplace environment when one works remotely. Remote work can create a thin line between personal and professional life, which demands that tools to balance the related areas have been devised. Let's discuss ways to preserve this balance by discussing productivity, stability, and physical and emotional health.

Productivity Consistency

Structured Routine: Establishing a regular daily schedule helps prepare for productive workdays. Setting consistent work hours and adhering to them makes maintaining a clear separation between work and personal time easier.

Designated Workspace: Having a separate workstation, free from interruptions, can create an environment where people can focus and be more productive. This physical separation within the home also signals to other household members that you are "working."

Breaks and Downtime: Taking short breaks during the workday helps prevent burnout and maintains high productivity levels. Methods like the Pomodoro Technique, which involves working for 25 minutes followed by a five-minute break, are commonly used to regain focus and energy throughout the day.

Physical Health

Ergonomic Setup: An investment in a comfortable and ergonomically correct workstation is essential. Chair back support, monitor height, and the appropriate keyboard placement can help to avoid strain or injury.

Regular Exercise: It's important to include physical activity in your daily routine. Whether it's a morning workout, an afternoon walk, or evening yoga, regular exercise helps reduce stress, improve mood, and enhance overall health.

Healthy Eating Habits: Though remote work easily allows access to the kitchen, following a balanced diet and sticking to fixed mealtimes is necessary. It is needed as an energy provider.

Mental Health

Social Interaction and Networking: Remote work can lead to feelings of isolation. Maintaining a social life is crucial, which can be done in various ways, such as virtual coffee breaks with colleagues or attending professional networking events. Additionally, spending time with friends and family can help combat isolation.

Mindfulness and Relaxation Techniques: Some practices that relieve stress include meditation, deep breathing exercises, and practicing mindfulness. Making time for such practices can aid in maintaining a balanced and serene mind.

Setting Boundaries: Communicating your availability and working schedule to colleagues and clients is essential. This helps manage expectations and reduces the pressure of being constantly available. Similarly, setting work boundaries with household members is crucial for maintaining focus and efficiency.

Professional Mental Health Support: Organizations can make a meaningful contribution by offering resources on mental health, counseling services, or wellness programs. Instilling an atmosphere where employees feel they can ask for help is vital.

The Impact on Company Culture

The shift to remote work has significant implications for organizational culture. This intangible yet critical aspect shapes the social fabric of a company. As more companies transition from traditional offices to remote or hybrid setups, there's a need to redefine company culture, reassess values, and adjust communication norms and employee engagement policies. This section explores how company culture has evolved in response to remote work (Webber et al., 2010).

Redefining Interaction and Communication

Virtual Communication Channels: In the virtual workplace, there needs to be more watercooler moments and impromptu hallway chats that naturally come up in physical offices. Companies are embracing digital platforms to ensure better communication and preserve a sense of community. These include regular video calls, virtual team-building activities, and online social events that help to maintain interpersonal ties and create a sense of belonging among remote teams.

Transparent and Frequent Communication: In a distant milieu, too much communication is preferable to not enough. Ongoing, clear, transparent, and frequent updates from the leadership about the company's goals, achievements, and pitfalls help maintain alignment and enrich trust. Simple town hall meetings, newsletters, and open Q&A's with the leadership all serve vital roles in information transfer to the workforce.

Fostering Inclusion and Belonging

Inclusive Culture in a Remote Setting: For the newcomers working away at home, distancing inadvertently creates a detachment or isolation from the office milieu. To build an inclusive culture, one needs to put a lot of effort into it by introducing the new employees virtually through onboarding processes that promote the company's values and norms and connect them with already-experienced colleagues via mentorship programs.

Recognition and Appreciation: Celebrating others' milestones, personal events, and achievements is essential for morale. Virtual shout-outs, award ceremonies, and acknowledgment in all company meetings can make sure that the employees are valued and recognized, even when this is done virtually.

Maintaining Engagement and Productivity

Results-Oriented Culture: Remote work changes the emphasis from time spent behind a desk to the real results and deliverables. Achieving a results-driven culture involves goal alignment, feedback management, and a trust approach to leadership. This change can encourage more autonomy, where employees own their work.

Continuous Learning and Development: Investing in employee development is even more critical because physical training workshops and conferences are no longer options. Many continuing education opportunities, such as online courses, virtual workshops, and webinars, will help keep the staff qualified while striving to work.

Challenges and Opportunities

Maintaining Company Identity: In a rural environment, reinforcing the organization's mission is challenging but ultimately essential. It is imperative that rituals and traditions, even if they are virtualized to some extent, can also help sustain a sense of belonging.

Adapting Leadership Styles: Leadership and management styles must be changed depending on the remote angle. This may include more proactive check-ins, an open digital channel policy, and a compassionate approach to the personal circumstances of every employee.

Needed Strategies for Fostering Cohesion

Promoting unity in a remote work setting is crucial because it keeps the team strong, united, and productive. Without co-location, deliberate strategies are required to foster a sense of belonging and shared purpose. This section discusses various ways of fostering team cohesion for remote workers.

1. Regular and Structured Communication

Scheduled Check-Ins: It is advisable to organize regular team meetings and one-on-ones to synchronize their performance. These meetings should combine professional stages and personal updates to create a comprehensive team atmosphere.

Open Channels of Communication: Support the implementation of collaborative technologies that promote spontaneous interaction, similar to unscripted discussions in a conventional workplace. Such interaction can be achieved through platforms such as Slack or Microsoft Teams.

2. Developing a Culture of Trust and Openness is Very Important

Empowerment and Autonomy: Give them autonomy and trust your team members a lot. In a remote environment, micromanagement undermines trust. Instead, concentrate more on the results and offer assistance when necessary.

Transparent Leadership: Leadership should openly inform the team of where the company is headed and its struggles and triumphs. This visibility builds up a feeling of safety and belonging, ensuring the team members feel appreciated and part of something larger than themselves.

3. Virtual Team-Building Activities

Regular Social Events: Plan virtual coffee sessions, happy hours, or team activities. These activities facilitate the elimination of formal barriers and allow for informal networking, much as socializing is very common in an office.

Recognition and Celebrations: We have to go out. The culture is supported by individuals and teams recognizing their respective successes.

4. Promoting Collaboration and Cross-Team Engagement

Project-Based Collaboration: Promote inter-team project collaboration. This mobilizes different talents and gives the team members a chance to work and learn from their peers drawn outside of their departments.

Cross-Training Sessions: Arrange knowledge-sharing or cross-training classes where the team members can share their experiences with others and learn from them. This creates an environment of great learning and respect.

5. Supporting Work-Life Balance

Respect Boundaries: Request the employees to create and uphold work-life boundaries. Try to avoid holding the meetings at odd times and remember that the personal time of team members is reserved for other activities.

Wellness Programs: Employ the programs or resources that promote mind and body wellness. This may include online fitness classes, mental health days off, or counseling services.

6. Personalized Communication and Feedback

Tailored Communication: Appreciate and accommodate unique communication styles and preferences. Some team members may choose video calls; others prefer emails or instant messaging.

Constructive Feedback: Provide regular, constructive feedback. Employees should also be encouraged to speak regularly about the work environment and culture.

Conclusion

As we explore remote work changes, we see it goes beyond just where we work. It's a significant shift in how we think about work. This chapter looks at remote work's trends, facts, pros, and cons, plus how to balance work and life and build company culture from afar.

We learn that remote work offers many benefits like flexibility, more productivity, saving money, finding talent worldwide, and helping the environment. But it also brings challenges like communication issues, trouble separating work from home, keeping data safe, managing performance, and dealing with fairness.

To tackle these challenges, we must focus on good communication, trust, openness in virtual teams, and building company culture. These steps show how we adapt and remain productive and connected even as work changes.

Chapter 4: Shifting Job Markets

The workforce is currently facing a big moment where technology and global patterns mix. This chapter discusses how the job market constantly changes because of new technology and international trends. Industries are redefined, and job roles are evolving quickly because technology is changing fast.

In this fast-changing environment, new skills become valuable once necessary skills become less functional. This chapter doesn't just discuss how job roles are changing; it also looks at the bigger picture of how work is changing and who benefits from these changes.

We'll discuss how some people adapt to these changes while others struggle. This chapter tells a story of change and explores the forces shaping future job markets. It's an invitation to understand the details of what's happening in the business world right now.

Job Market Trends in the Digital Age

Today, work is undergoing a profound transformation alongside the digital revolution, with new technologies shaping the future job market. These changes are interconnected, reshaping both the nature and direction of work.

The rise of virtual communication, spurred by developments like cloud computing and video conferencing, has redefined where and how work is done. Events like the global COVID-19 pandemic have accelerated this shift, emphasizing the importance of achieving a balance between work and personal life.

The gig economy has also emerged, with platforms like Uber and Airbnb offering short-term freelance opportunities. This trend values diverse experiences over traditional career progression.

Employers now prioritize specialized skills over basic qualifications, leading to a focus on lifelong learning and micro-credentials. AI and automation are changing the job landscape, creating opportunities but also displacing traditional roles.

This tech-driven era increasingly values soft skills such as creativity and adaptability. Sustainability and social responsibility are also shaping job markets, leading to the rise of "green jobs" and positions focused on corporate social responsibility.

In this data-driven age, numeracy and critical thinking skills are essential for navigating the job market. Overall, the modern workforce must possess technical expertise, soft skills, and flexibility to thrive in a constantly evolving environment.

1. Data Literacy: One of the most essential elements of employing data in data-driven organizations is interpreting and analyzing data to arrive at conclusions.

2. Cybersecurity Expertise: Cyber threats continue increasing with increased cyber-terrorism, cybercrimes, and cyber-attacks, as well as the emergence of cyber warfare techniques. This makes the knowledge of achieving secure networks and systems to become important.

3. Software Development: In coding and software system development skills, particularly languages like Java, Python, and Javascript.

4. AI and Machine Learning: Achieving this is crucial in allowing businesses to innovate while enhancing efficiency. Therefore, the designing of algorithms is the best way to do so.

Hard skills such as computer literacy, data analysis, and data management are also essential, and you can only do with soft skills such as emotional intelligence, critical thinking, creativity, innovation, adaptability, and flexibility. Digital literacy concerning digitally engaged content, understanding various technology literacy skills, and project management skills such as agile methodology and organizational skills are a must. Additionally, most newly emerging knowledge and skill requirements, namely sustainability and ethical competencies such as environmental consciousness and ethical reasoning, are gaining prominence, particularly in AI.

However, it's not just about individual skills. There's a growing need for a multidisciplinary approach to problem-solving. Professionals must stay updated on these changes and continually improve their skills to remain relevant in a competitive job market driven by digitalization. Employers prioritize nurturing these competencies to boost innovation, ensure stability, and stay adaptable in a fast-paced labor market.

Emerging Industries and Job Opportunities

Globalization and rapid technological advancements drive significant changes in various industries, creating new opportunities for businesses and employment. Industries are evolving to address future challenges and emphasize elements that shape the world of tomorrow.

The renewable energy sector is experiencing substantial growth due to the urgent need to address climate change and reduce fossil fuel consumption. This industry utilizes diverse energy sources such as sunlight, wind, hydroelectric power, bioenergy, and advancements in energy storage technologies like batteries.

The demand for automation and intelligent services is rising among businesses and consumers, fueled by advancements in Artificial Intelligence (AI) and Machine Learning (ML). These technologies find applications in various fields, including medical image analysis, automated customer support, and advanced supply chain management.

Biotechnology and genomics revolutionize sectors like medicine, agriculture, and scientific research. Rapid advancements in personalized medicine, led by technologies like CRISPR-Cas9, are transforming healthcare and agriculture, offering new possibilities in genetic engineering and synthetic biology.

Cybersecurity rapidly expands to protect our interconnected lives, where personal information, homes, structures, and companies are all linked. This industry continually evolves to defend against threats and build a secure cyber infrastructure capable of preventing and responding to emerging risks.

The increasing urbanization demand for eco-friendly cities drives the growing focus on sustainable and innovative city solutions. Utilizing technologies like the Internet of Things (IoT), cities aim to enhance urban life, boosting productivity while prioritizing environmental friendliness and sustainability.

The Health and Wellness industry is experiencing significant growth, fueled partly by an aging population requiring attention to health conditions. Additionally, there's a broader societal focus on overall well-being. This diverse industry spans pharmaceuticals, medical supplies, self-care products, mental wellness services, and telemedicine, among others.

Through Edtech and Online Learning, AI is revolutionizing education with platforms and virtual classrooms tailored to individual needs, essential for continuous learning in a competitive job market.

FinTech is reshaping finance, offering new ways to manage money with online banking, mobile payments, and peer-to-peer lending, transforming traditional financial services.

Space exploration, once dominated by governments, now sees private companies entering the field, offering satellite services, space tourism, and the potential for asteroid mining.

AgriTech and Food Innovation address global food sustainability challenges with technology-driven solutions like precision farming and alternative protein production, aiming to meet food demands without harming the planet.

These industries shape the future, prompting other sectors to adapt to changing global demands and technological advancements, opening up new opportunities for innovation and growth.

The Gig Economy and Flexible Work Arrangements

In the modern world, the gig economy has assumed a noticeable prominence in the last decade. It has engendered a revolution in the labor market and national economics with the preference for contracts that last for a limited period and freelance jobs. This change towards more liquid and fluid forms of work brings a multiplex construct that reshapes the dynamics of labor markets, re-shapes and re-structures the labor force, and affects patterns of economic activities in more profound and broader ways.

The gig economy provides workers a lot of flexibility in the job market. They can choose when and where to work and easily switch between different employers. This flexibility allows them to balance their work with other commitments in life, like education or personal interests. With the gig economy, location is not a barrier, so people can work from anywhere, whether traveling, preferring a nomadic lifestyle, or like to work from home. This setup lets individuals explore different career paths across various industries, creating a diverse professional portfolio. Additionally, the gig economy encourages entrepreneurship, as gig work can serve as a starting point for building brands or launching new ventures.

Another widening of the talent pool that the gig economy creates is the delivery of a global talent pool. Employers are driven far beyond the geographical limitations of the local job market. They can scout the best talents worldwide by differentiating cultures and intellectual dimensions to deliver better, high-quality services and products in innovative designs. A key advantage of employing freelancers is that one can get access to skills within niche areas such that an organization may hire a freelancer with specialized skills or when a one-off project is needed in its development, especially for small firms or start-ups that require specific skills at various times in their developments. This flexible and scalable model makes it possible for companies to change their workforce unprecedentedly according to fluctuating market conditions.

The gig economy benefits businesses economically by reducing the expenses associated with maintaining physical workspaces and providing employee benefits. This helps lower the overall labor costs for companies. In the gig economy, workers are often paid based on their performance, which ensures a fair distribution of company revenues and encourages them to work more efficiently.

Gig work also offers income opportunities for individuals, either as a supplementary source of income or as a pathway to traditional employment. This is particularly valuable for those facing challenges in traditional job markets. Additionally, gig work contributes to local economies by bringing in revenue, which supports economic growth and resilience, especially in regions with high unemployment rates.

In the gig economy, teams comprise individuals with diverse skills who continuously educate themselves. These workers, often known as side hustlers, are innovative and take on various projects to broaden their skill sets and gain insights across different industries. Their ability to adapt makes them highly desirable to employers, and they often pursue a portfolio career approach, showcasing a collection of diverse work experiences as a valuable asset.

In this fast-paced gig economy, workers must quickly adapt to market demands and stay competitive by constantly enhancing their skills through online courses, workshops, and certifications. Understanding the latest technologies and digital tools is essential, as many gig opportunities require knowledge of specific software or platforms.

The gig economy is changing the traditional employment model by emphasizing flexibility, agility, and access to a highly skilled workforce. It significantly impacts various aspects of work life, including global economies and career advancement. It continues to shape the future of work in significant ways.

Challenges and Considerations

The gig economy brings benefits but also drawbacks that affect job security and raise concerns for workers, society, and regulators. These challenges ripple across industries, disrupting traditional sectors and creating a supportive environment for the gig economy.

One major issue is the need for job security. Gig workers often need long-term contracts, leading to financial instability and insecurity. They miss out on benefits like health insurance and retirement plans, which threatens their financial and personal well-being in the long run.

Uneven incomes are another problem. Gig workers may struggle to predict their earnings, leading to financial uncertainty. As competition increases and rates decrease, it becomes harder to secure consistent work, creating a feast-or-famine situation for many workers.

Achieving the work-life equilibrium on the grounds of the economy can have many variables. However, this kind of work is quite flexible, which can confuse the line between work and family because there is no clear boundary between work and home. Worse, employees may feel that they have to work all the time. Even though it is not valid, they are right. Seeking the next job and the void of precise work hours make for health crises that translate into both mental and physical health sufferings.

Other challenges that make their way through the gig economy revolve around regulations and laws. The classification of gig workers as employees or independent contractors is ambiguous. It plays a vital role in many aspects relating to their privileges. It suits social security benefits so that taxation becomes effective. Most of the time, this results in disagreements and court sittings on the rights, protections, and benefits that the workers ought to enjoy under various regulatory regimens.

The gig economy has brought about both disruptions and new opportunities for industries. Companies like Uber, Lyft, and Airbnb have transformed sectors like transportation and travel, focusing on demand-based services and consumer-driven environments. This competition pushes traditional companies to innovate and improve their services, ultimately raising the overall quality of service in the market. Additionally, other industries, such as retail and food and beverage, have adopted the gig economy model, leading to changes in employment structures.

Moreover, the growth of supporting industries has been driven by the needs of the gig economy. More online platforms and apps have emerged to match freelancers with gigs, and freelancing has expanded into niche areas such as home-based jobs. Payment processing technology has adapted to accommodate gig workers' irregular earnings patterns, leading to convenient and secure payment solutions. Services like co-working spaces and dedicated insurance packages have also emerged to meet the specific needs of gig workers, indicating the emergence of a niche market tailored to this workforce.

Future Implications

The phenomenal growth of the gig economy is sure to trigger debate and to observe requests for review and regulations to deal with the specific issues and opportunities that this represents. The ongoing trend toward regulation, combined with gig work integration with traditional employment, is rendering the workplace landscape and causing a cultural change in the conception and practice of work.

As for new possible regulations, there is an increasing tendency to improve the rights and protection of an ordinary worker in the gig economy. People like the owners of the said companies understand that stakeholders are pushing for additional laws to guarantee that gig workers get good treatment and rights equal to those traditional employees enjoy. Workers' rights include fair wages, availing of benefits, and protections against wrongful dismissals or other forms of abuse. That is, this aim is to close the gap in the benefits, which entails that those gig workers will have a separate safety net just like that present in traditional jobs.

Points of attention also include taxation and compliance. Governments and regulatory bodies acknowledge that it is necessary to reformat the existing preparation of the tax system so that it can cover gig workers who are unique compared to other citizens. This includes ensuring the correct taxing of gig income and creating clear rules for legal compliance in addressing problems such as worker characterization and revenue contribution, which is well-known by competent authorities in some countries.

The blending of gig work with traditional employment has led to the emergence of new hybrid working models. Companies are blurring the lines between gig and regular jobs by offering flexible working hours and locations, allowing employees to take on full-time or part-time roles in project-based contexts. Similarly, individuals are pursuing internal gigs alongside their primary jobs, giving them access to a broader range of job opportunities and allowing them to adapt to the dynamic demands of the market. This trend also provides opportunities for personal development and growth.

Moreover, there is a notable shift in cultural attitudes toward work. The focus on work-life balance, job satisfaction, and career diversity reshapes the labor market into a more dynamic and fluid environment. Long-term employment is becoming less rigid, with people increasingly open to transitioning between gig work and traditional jobs as they seek diverse experiences and personal fulfillment. This cultural shift reflects a broader societal trend toward valuing flexibility, autonomy, and meaningful contributions in the workplace.

Conclusion

This chapter marks the beginning of our journey through the changing landscape of job markets, influenced by technology and global shifts. We looked at how the digital age alters job expectations and skills needed in today's society. Our research uncovered new industry trends with diverse job opportunities and requirements, signaling a move towards skill-based markets.

We also explored the gig economy and its impact on work arrangements as more people seek flexibility and independence. While this shift offers personal and professional growth opportunities, it also presents challenges like securing stability and embracing lifelong learning.

Overall, workplaces are undergoing transformative changes, reshaping industries and norms. Professionals, employers, and policymakers must adapt, learn continuously, and plan. Developing adaptable skills and creating agile workforces are vital for success in these dynamic job markets. As we navigate this new age, the future holds uncertainties and boundless possibilities for those prepared to embrace change.

Chapter 5: The Future of Skills

Right now, we're seeing big changes in how people work. Skills that used to guarantee success are becoming outdated because of fast-paced technology and global changes. Things that used to be important in our personal and work lives might not be helpful anymore. We need to learn new skills to keep up with the changes happening in the job world.

In the last chapter, we discussed skills that will be important for the future. Now, let's go deeper and see why things like understanding technology, thinking critically, and being able to adapt are so important for doing well in today's jobs. These skills aren't just ideas; they're significant for success at work.

This chapter will provide practical tips and ideas for learning these important skills and show you how to adjust to the changes in the job world right now.

Essential Skills for the Future

Today, digital literacy is the fundamental component of digital competence, reflecting not merely specific computer skills but relatively comprehensive knowledge and abilities in handling various digital tools and environments that shape everything around modern daily life (Marr, 2022).

It should not be doubted that Cloud Computing Proficiency is a key element of digital literacy. It manages the cloud solutions for data storage, workflows, and computing. However, the capability to perform operations in major cloud platforms such as AWS, Google Cloud, or Microsoft Azure gives individuals and businesses access to scalable resources that aid in better optimization and innovation (Marr, 2022).

Then social media savviness is another factor that should be considered. In a technology-advanced world, social media platforms are necessary for marketing, networking, and brand designing and development, so professional competence in such platforms is inevitable. Not that using these platforms is admirable, but how well one uses them to communicate and put across brand messages to many different people in a diverse audience (Marr, 2022).

Digital communication tools and fluent skills are critical for effective communication in remote and hybrid workplaces. The resolution of this task requires using tools similar to Slack, Microsoft Teams, Zoom, or Asana; the software makes team collaboration possible. In addition to mastery of these tools, it is vital to know how to behave appropriately and comply with the best restrictions of online communication to keep an appropriate level of professionalism and ensure a clear and compelling conversation in a virtual environment (Phrase Structure Swap).

In today's world, where information is said to be in excess, data literacy has become the desired ability. Data interpretation, analysis, and valuable insight generation are in demand because the ability to interpret what data means is valuable. This encompasses more than just skills in applying data visualization tools as well as analytics software to transform the vast, complicated data sets into information that is legible and can be used without fear; evaluating the sources of the data is a critical part as well which assures only credible, reliable information used for decisions.

In the same way, in creating some data insights, communication of this information is as equally crucial as drawing its diagram. Communicating the results obtained in a study using data effectively and powerfully through reports, presentations, and visualizations is essential. It ensures that insights are not only due but translatable, thus driving informed conclusions within the organization.

It can be concluded that digital and data literacy are wanted qualities and necessary elements relevant to digital time. They include a wide range of skills, from being adept in the undertaking of cloud computing and having a solid knowledge of social media to mastery of digital communication gadgets and skills in interpreting data and politics. In the digital era, these skills will be woven into the core of individual and organizational success, and their relevance will triumph as the world becomes more data-driven and interconnected.

Technological Adaptability

Adaptability becomes an essential tool in the future as the technology landscape keeps changing, which makes man adaptable, not simply change accompanying the current pattern, but venture into future innovations. Technological adaptability includes a variety of skills and habits that allow people and businesses to have the skills and perspective to use and implement technology in a changing world.

Only when there is the practice of continuous learning and curiosity is technological adaptability. One of the ways of growing a culture of constant learning, which needs to be encouraged in the domain where discoveries are appearing as fast as the time of year flight, is cultivating youthful curiosity toward new technologies. This focus on development and learning means other mechanics will go out of their way to know what is happening by enrolling in courses, attending webinars, reading industry publications, and participating in practical sessions. This is because staying informed and updating oneself on learning new things daily ensures that the individuals and the organization are proactive with technological change.

Adaptive by quick adaptation to new technologies is another essential aspect of adaptability. It is not just about adapting to new tools or systems but about putting well-designed innovative solutions into practical use in the current workflow. This agility requires careful consideration and sensible weighing, determining new technologies' value and practicability, ramifications, and compliance with the organizational objectives. The foundation for a competitive edge is the willingness to experiment, take conscious and intelligent risks, and harness the ability to change inherent to new technology. It drives an innovative vision of strategy and creating environmentally sustainable value.

The primary factor is resilience to technological change. With technology, specific changes and challenges are bound to come, as changes could be viewed as disruptions. As the concept to be focused on here, resilience is much more than simply surviving these transitions. It is understanding them as opportunities for advancement, innovation, and creativity. This includes identifying and managing problems and disturbances resulting from innovation and technology advancement, where strategies are to be adjusted when necessary, as well as a future focus. It's about looking at every obstacle not as a defeat but as a learning, improvement, and creative problem-solving catalyst.

Critical Thinking

Critical thinking is the foundation for successful problem-solving and decision-making. It is an integral process of a disciplined and systematic procedure for comprehending and assessing information. It is a multi-component ability, central to the final solution of complex issues and the correct decision.

Skills in analyzing a text are crucial for critical thinking. They involve breaking down complex problems or ideas into smaller, more manageable parts. This systematic approach helps people understand issues better and address them more effectively. By analyzing problems, individuals can dissect their components, examine their structure, and know how they are interconnected. This careful examination is essential for unraveling complex issues, identifying underlying patterns, and deriving structured solutions.

A critical thinker should be observant and able to think independently. It encompasses the ability to resist the temptations to groupthink and follow a collective mindset with one built on our logic, evidence-based reasoning, and rational, solid analysis. In dependent-minded thinking, information is simply taken at face value. At the same time, independent thinkers question underlying assumptions, evaluate evidence, and draw conclusions based on solid reasoning. Such a tendency to think independently is critical in driving innovations into our lives, challenging the validity of the established status, and proposing new alternative, sometimes revolutionary thoughts in the discussions and decision-making processes.

This requirement results in influential critical thinkers possessing a solution-oriented Type Mindset. They are more than problem spotters; they can also develop practical solutions for the problems. This involves an outcome-focused orientation and a structured method to clarify what underpins the issues. Critical thinkers are the best at identifying problems accurately, evaluating the factors that contributed to the problem, and then finding a practical, well-crafted solution. Their method is not concerned solely with diagnostic purposes but with constructive ways to make things right.

Creativity and Innovation

This encompasses divergent thinking, a critical aspect of creativity and innovation. The looseness allows one to create multiple alternatives to the solution to the problem or case faced. This type of thought involves venturing into the range of unconventional political processes, bending the rules of other already set paragons, and breaking out of the box. Divergent thinking is an indispensable transcription of innovativeness and problem-solving, where exploring versatile options yields immeasurable creativity and vigor to newfound solutions.

The other necessary domain for creative and innovative thinking is connecting disparate ideas. It is the ability to find patterns, establish relationships between apparently dissociated concepts, and combine them to produce new value. Such ability to produce original synthesis by combining and recombining ideas from several domains might give rise to brilliant inventions and discoveries that nobody has seen before and direct to new solutions and ways.

Risk-taking and Experimentation are essential components of the creation process, which does not require a single explanation. Innovators and innovators know that ideas are different from success. Still, they see perseverance in failed attempts as a valuable thing. They appreciate failure as an integral part of the creative process, treating it as a means of gaining knowledge, boosting one's potential, and honing concepts. This attitude promotes a culture of trial and error, wherein the risk is calculated and is considered a critical aspect of the progress toward innovation and finding unexplored possessions.

Continuous improvement and iteration emphasize that creativity and innovation are not one-time events but involve kinetic processes. The innovation process is continuous as it does not include only one activity but rather a series of steps of refinement and development. That is why it can be noted that winsome innovations stand as a consequence of continuous efforts to improve concepts or products to change with the times grouped with self-sufficient tuition. By making this iterative approach, crafting such creative acts never stops but continues to thrive, develop, and increase to fit the needs of new perils and possibilities.

Emotional Intelligence (EI)

This topic encompasses critical elements of effective interpersonal communication and effective and impactful leadership, all of which contribute to one's overall well-being. It centers on emotional intelligence, a multidimensional competency that includes self-awareness, self-control, motivation, sensitivity, and interpersonal competence. These competencies constitute social skills and develop harmonious social relations.

There is no higher importance factor than self-awareness, an indispensable element of emotional intelligence. It requires an in-depth knowledge and perception of an individual's emotional intelligence, understanding one's strengths, weaknesses, and values, and recognizing the effects of these internal states on the whole society. A person who is aware of himself- or herself, in terms of cognitive processing, is in tune with their feelings and how they can control them because they influence their thoughts and behaviors. As a result, this introspective instrument motivates these individuals towards a substantial life orientation and the realization of their impact on other people.

Self-regulation is the individual's ability to control emotions and impulses with the help of proper self-regulation. Self-regulators have the potential to control or modify their emotional reactions with this ability. They can avoid doing impulsive things or engaging in actions influenced by their mood, which might result in improperness or be too harmful. Through this skill, people can build their good judgment, remain professional uncertainties, and adapt to sudden changes in a patient's medical condition in a positive way.

In Emotional Intelligence, motivation is not limited to material rewarding elements such as money or prestige. The meaning of my answer to this question is the quality of determination that drives us to set objectives and pursue them with intensity and perseverance. Motivated people are generally positive, work hard towards their goals, and never back down when defeated. This statement can be true because these people show zeal and passion in their work; therefore, they become role models for other people.

Social skills are embedded in emotional intelligence, the final output resulting from being able to communicate with others. People with high social skills also report the best input in initiating a relationship, establishing rapport, and identifying common ground with different groups. They are excellent communicators and well-oriented to networking, conflict resolution, and cooperation needs. In teams and leadership positions, their art of social comfort and facility leaves little to be desired, and such people cannot be replaced easily.

Cultural Awareness and Diversity Management

For successful inclusive initiatives, global firms must expand profoundly and accommodate culturally diverse practices. As countries become increasingly interdependent, cultural diversity appreciation is vital in addressing social issues in the workplace; behavior that enables people to interact effectively and have healthy lives is an essential aspect of their work.

Cultural sensitivity is The primary basis for interacting effectively across cultural barriers. It entails awareness, respect, and acceptance of the differences in behavior, beliefs, and ways of doing things among the several cultures. Savvy people are keen to see small components of different cultural environments. They treat the cross-cultural communication process with respect, appreciating the various cultural differences and values in others. Remembering that people and institutions are culturally diverse, they can overcome misinterpretations and stereotypes, establish fruitful relationships, and promote the spirit of openness to differences.

In a global firm, Inclusive Communication is essential because people from different cultures and their diverse thoughts are united under one roof. Constructing an atmosphere of communicative inclusion implies considering and providing different cultural and linguistic subtleties to accelerate the process of inclusive communication in any case. It entails encouraging free-flowing conversation, listening intently to all sides without discrimination, and ensuring that individuals can be heard and understood. Inclusive communication cultivates a feeling of integration and esteem among team members. It boosts teamwork and similar factors to make the workplace enjoyable.

Leadership Skills

Given that the workings of workplaces will be different in the future and workplace hierarchies will change, it is even more critical to have efficient leaders. In this way, leadership, in a broad sense, goes beyond the typical practice of wielding power to inspire others and influence them back into acting together toward some common goals.

One of the hallmark traits of effective leadership is Visionary Thinking. It is an essential skill for developing a convincing picture, which allows me to give direction and influence others. Visionary leaders plan for the future. They make evidence-based decisions and foresee changes in their departments or organizations concerning evolving trends and challenges; these types of managers direct people toward what should be accomplished over time. Therefore, the clarity in every statement they make ensures comprehension when it comes to stating what collective and individual goals are and why these particular goals have been initiated for achievement. Visionary leaders are talented at creating a vision of an attractive future, inspiring their subordinates with a unifying cause, and directing the collective movement toward fulfilling that promise.

In Influential Leadership, the power of influence is more in the Credit-Control-Government model. These influential leaders use the process to take some of their credibility, competence, and interpersonal abilities, prompting high respect for them, thereby causing people around such individuals to act in specific ways. They realize that genuine leadership revolves around something other than power. Still, instead, it is about the creation of trust, respect, and working together. Influential leaders are active listeners and clear communicators and promote respectful relationships. They lead with sincere care for the welfare and growth of their subordinates while holding influence through connecting to people, understanding them, and being able to inspire.

Today, empowering others is an essential part of leadership. This includes creating an ecosystem of care and support, an environment where people feel appreciated, respected, and trustful; they make decisions in their field. On the other hand, empowering leaders orient employees toward developing skills in decision-making, creating a sense of ownership and allowing them to be autonomous. They equip members with what they need, orient them right, and motivate them but also allow liberally for maximizing the freedom to mine. Leadership empowerment is also an approach that increases the performance of individuals and team performance and fosters accountability, innovation, and continuous improvement.

Lifelong Learning and Self-Motivation

One of the essential components of lifelong learning is Proactive Learning. It is a process that involves identifying and searching for learning development opportunities and being ready to learn from new experiences. Proactive learners take advantage of opportunities. Still, they discover different educational channels, including training sessions or course registration, and keep up to date with the current trends in their respective fields. They are always trying to improve their competence and increase their depth of knowledge. This method makes them contemporary in their field, take the lead, and make innovations.

The other key ingredient in lifelong learning is self-motivation. It includes previous analysis of personal goals; it demands a high standard degree of discipline and commitment in achieving professional plus individual development. Self-motivated learners are always eager to learn and strive for self-perfection. They are dedicated to their path of learning. They overcome difficulties and try again after failures. Most of their motivations are generally from having a genuine love for the industry, being interested in learning more about it, and wanting, just like anybody would be attracted to, to put their learned skills to valuable use.

Flexibility and Adaptability

In this age of swift changes and volatile tremors, adaptability has become a fundamental skill imperative to survive the intricacies and opportunities afforded by today's world.

Acceptance characterizes adaptability. It relates to looking at change not as a hindrance but as an avenue for progress, success, and advancement. Flexible people and companies regard a transition as a stimulator that can put them ahead and create additional opportunities. They have the adaptability to change strategies and approaches as situations develop. By incorporating change, they remain both timely and competitive, and adaptable, thereby minimizing possible threats and turning them into opportunities for success.

Another vital phenomenon of adaptability is Adaptive Problem-Solving. This requires that problems be undertaken with an open attitude and engaging in a variety of solution alternatives. Adaptive problem solvers follow different patterns or frameworks but, on the contrary, are prepared to use innovative and non-standard methods for solving problems. They know that the best answers usually come with an iterative approach through experimenting, learning by errors, and reacting to new evidence. Such a flexible style of finding a justification for actions helps them navigate complexities and challenges, resulting in efficient, novel solutions.

Lifelong Learning and Continuous Skill Development

With the era of intensive technological advances and variable labor markets, lifelong learning and development now appear as essential aspects that help to remain personally relevant and promote social progress in The Future of Lifelong Learning and Work 2008. There is also no way to underestimate the necessity of accepting a lifelong learning and professional development approach. Let us touch upon the importance of lifelong learning in at least a minor detail.

In a time when sectors are evolving and new technology keeps redefining positions in the job sector, Staying Relevant in the Job Market is essential. First and foremost, the skills that are popular today can quickly become worthless in a year or two because of new technological innovations and market demands (The Future of Lifelong Learning and Work, 2008).

Keeping up with technological advances is crucial to remaining relevant in today's fast-paced world. Each field undergoes consistent changes due to technology, and lifelong learning helps people remain up-to-date with the newest tools, platforms, or trends.

Another vital advantage of lifelong learning is that it fosters creativity and innovation. This inflow of ideas, knowledge, and exposure creates the environment for developing creative instincts, which are based on imagination. This ultimately leads to innovative solutions in products or processes.

Increasing personal satisfaction and well-being are ideals that cannot be measured empirically. Yet, lifelong learning is thought to bring this intrinsic value. Continuous learning is essential in personal development and self-actualization, hence increased levels of satisfaction with life as well as a sense of achievement.

Building Resilience in a Changing World

Lifelong learning promotes adaptability and resilience, enabling people to better deal with change and unpredictability. People dedicated to learning can better face challenges and get through transitional stages.

Contributing to Society and the Economy

From a broader perspective, LLL's culture promotes societal development and economic growth. Its educated and skilled workforce spurs innovation, increases efficiency, and makes it possible to find solutions for contemporary complex problems. Realizing the need to promote lifelong learning and continuous skill enhancement creates a platform for enabling an environment that encourages ongoing education.

Constant skill development is a purposeful and dynamic process that allows for success in the modern marketplace. To sustain this uninterrupted growth, there is a need to implement well-planned tactics in learning and development. Here are some strategies for

Continuous Skill Development

Set Clear Goals and Objectives: Identify your areas of deficiency based on your job or life goals. By setting practical learning goals, you can set a direction and a purpose for where you want to go next. Create a personalized learning plan. Draft a study plan based on these goals, considering how much time you can set aside for learning. Whether you're planning for a schedule that includes online courses, workshops, or less conventional modes such as horizontal learning, always keep it flexible while being structured enough to avoid losing sight of your objective.

Leverage Online Learning Platform: Use the wealth of online learning resources available today. Websites such as Coursera,

Udemy, LinkedIn Learning, and Khan Academy offer a wide array of courses in whatever you're interested in.

Engage in Continuous Professional Development (CPD): Attend industry-specific training, workshops, conferences, or webinars. CPD activities help you keep abreast of changes in your profession and the latest tools and techniques practitioners use. Practice and apply your skills. The application of knowledge is the maximization of learning. Look for a company project, freelancing initiatives, or volunteer activities where you can apply the newly acquired skills.

Seek Feedback and Reflect: Feedback is the beauty of growth. Regularly seek feedback from peers, mentors, or supervisors and create time to reflect on how you're evolving with time, the challenges you faced, and your learning experiences.

Foster a Growth Mindset: Develop a psychological approach that welcomes challenges, is resilient in adversity and failure, and has the perseverance to not just learn but learn from mistakes. It is critical for future learning and development.

Build a Professional Network: Networking is not just a job-hunting tool. A network of professionals can lend emotional and professional support and give you cues toward any industry trends that can help you develop your competence. Stay curious. Cultivate interests beyond your field and across different disciplines. Keeping curiosity alive and being open to new ideas helps strengthen the hunger for knowledge and keeps it alive. Prioritize and manage your time. Good time management is essential for continuous learning. Hence, you should manage your learning activities well and ensure that all the professional developmental work doesn't come crashing behind other priorities.

Maintain a Work-Life-Study Balance: While continuous learning is beneficial, it's also essential to strike a balance, and doing so will prevent burnout, too. Give adequate time to rest as well as recreation. Soft skills play a vital role in the workplace as the nature of work changes all the time. Soft skills, also known as interpersonal or essential skills, are broad abilities that help one interact effectively with others, cope well with change, and function in complex social climates. They are increasingly becoming crucial to a successful career.

Enhance Team Collaboration: Soft skills such as communication, empathy, and conflict resolution are essential to building a collaborative workplace where people can work in teams, understand alternate viewpoints, and work amicably towards common goals.

Drive Leadership and Management Success: Leadership isn't just about being able to chart long-range thinking and decision-making; it should also mean inspiring others and leading teams. Soft leadership skills such as emotional intelligence, flexibility, and motivational abilities are essential for successful management.

Improve Customer Satisfaction and Service: Soft skills such as active listening, empathy, and problem-solving directly apply to roles that deal directly with customers. Understanding and responding to the customer's needs is critical to building trust and loyalty.

Facilitate Change Management: Change in today's workplace is constant, and soft skills are essential for dealing with and succeeding in adopting new technologies and procedures or changes at the organizational level.

Strengthen Problem-Solving Abilities: However, complex problem-solving seldom ever emerges from only technical skills; it is more intrinsic to creativity and systemic thinking. The multiple perspectives that soft skills open provide which problems can be approached and solutions from which problems can be developed.

Promote a Positive Workplace Culture: Very much the soft skills that are valued and are demonstrated in a good work environment. It enhances employee satisfaction and retention and helps attract the best talent.

Support Professional Growth and Career Progression: Individuals with solid and soft skills tend to advance in their careers. Such skills allow them to handle their responsibilities, be aware of the social dynamics present within their workplaces, and lead teams, making them powerfully in-demand candidates for promotions.

Enhance Communication Across the Organization: Good operational communication ensures that every idea or piece of information is not miscommunicated and that things run smoothly.

Build Resilience and Emotional Stability: Soft skills such as being able to deal with stress and self-regulation of emotions make people more adaptable, able to deal with the challenges that can come from a workplace, and exist in an emotionally balanced state to grow in both a personal and professional sense. The changing workplace landscape due to technological evolution, economic changes, and cultural trends emphasizes one thing: soft skills are now in higher demand than ever. People need technical skills and interpersonal and emotional competencies to create a working environment that supports collaboration and creativity, is fluid, and thrives on change. Here's an exploration of how soft skills play in the workplace as it undergoes metamorphosis.

Navigating Digital Communication

Traditional forms of communication have transformed, too. Good written communication is still a fundamental skill, as is the ability to apply empathy to understand the tone of digital messages, not to mention the correct application of digital etiquette. To keep up with the large-scale employee shift to digital-first workplace communication, here are ten essential soft skills every digital-first workplace communicator needs to learn:

Fostering Inclusivity and Diversity: A richer tapestry of individuals—different cultural, racial, and generational groups—are sharing working environments. Fostering inclusive, cohesive working groups demands emotional and cultural intelligence, a skill of increasing importance in ensuring team and company relations are respectful, compatible, supportive, and healthy.

Driving Innovation and Creativity: Creativity, openness, and adeptness at giving and receiving factual and constructive feedback are essential for creating an environment where new ideas are turned into realities.

Enhancing Employee Engagement and Retention: Staff who feel they are being listened to, understood, valued, and supported are likelier to feel engaged with their work. Leaders with soft skills such as compassion and solid communication are the architects of fantastic work cultures.

Facilitating Interdisciplinary Collaboration: Practices as soft skills allow individuals to bridge disparate disciplines of expertise, ensuring collaboration in executing teamwork masterpieces.

Supporting Conflict Resolution and Negotiation: Negotiation is the soft skill that facilitates the resolution of problems arising from interpersonal conflict, ensuring that they result in a positive outcome.

Leading Through Change: The ability to adapt to change, resilience in bouncing back, and the capacity for empathetic inspiration are crucial soft skills that good leaders need to process change with grace and confidence.

Building Professional Networks: Networking is more than the trading of business cards. At its heart, networking is structured around mutual goals, facilitated by soft skills like interpersonal communication, team prosody, and professional courtesy.

Promoting Lifelong Learning and Development: The goal of any learning organization is to sustain a growth mindset characterized by a passion for curiosity, an intrinsic urge to self-motivate, and the ability to navigate toward insight and innovation.

Conclusion

As we wrap up Chapter 5, it's evident that the world of work is changing rapidly, requiring us to adapt and develop new skills. We discussed the importance of future-proof skills like adaptability and critical thinking, which are essential for navigating an ever-changing environment.

We emphasized the need for lifelong learning and continuous skill development. With skills quickly becoming outdated, we must keep learning and growing. Lifelong learning isn't just a professional obligation but a personal necessity for fostering creativity and adaptability.

We also delved into soft skills, highlighting their significance in modern workplaces. Human skills like empathy and teamwork become even more valuable as technology advances. These skills foster innovation, diversity, and team cohesion.

As we look to the future, skills are both a challenge and an opportunity. It's essential for individuals to adopt a growth mindset and for organizations to create environments that support skill development. By embracing lifelong learning and nurturing human relationships, we can adapt to the ever-changing world and unlock our full potential. Together, we can create a resilient, adaptive future filled with opportunities for growth and fulfillment.

Chapter 6: Adapting to Technological Disruption

In today's fast-paced business world, waiting for things to happen can be deadly. Companies need to take action and adapt quickly to survive. This chapter gives you a behind-the-scenes look at companies that have thrived despite disruptions. They didn't just go with the flow of technological changes; they used them to innovate and grow.

But this isn't just a story about how amazing these companies are. It's about understanding how to prepare for significant changes. A big part of that is being a disruptor – someone who sees changes coming and develops intelligent strategies to use new technologies like cloud AI, IoTs, and blockchain to improve their business.

From now on, I'll focus on agility, vision, and adaptability in my case studies. This chapter is your guide to navigating constant change and running a successful business in today's ever-changing world. Welcome to Chapter 6!

Anticipating and Embracing Change

The modern business world requires people to predict and welcome change. It is about surviving, but even more so than taking advantage of opportunities while setting a trail for innovation growth. With technological disruption continuing to change industries, proactivity in adapting is a key differentiator (Armstrong, 2023). Here are strategies for effectively anticipating change:

Foster a Culture of Curiosity and Learning

This initiative is essential for all organizations that want to remain dynamic and relevant to maintain a culture of curiosity and constant learning. Here are ways to foster this culture:

Encourage Questioning and Exploration: Create a culture that encourages inquiries and questions team members ask, assumptions they can challenge, and uncertainties they can explore without fear of censure or failure.

Provide Learning Resources and Opportunities: Provide opportunities to take the courses online and offer workshops, seminars, and conferences. Challenge workers to develop personal development plans and plan for the development of other workers to share knowledge in the future.

Implement Knowledge Sharing Platforms: Create channels for the employees to share the lessons learned, the information regarding their industry, and the learning they get from interacting with the people around them.

Set Learning Goals and Incentives: Incorporate goals into performance analysis and reward or celebrate successes in this area. This highlights that lifelong learning is appreciated and recognized.

Invest in Market Research: Market dynamics and consumer behavior are essential to comprehend change.

Here's how organizations can effectively invest in market research:

Conduct Regular Industry Analysis: Regularly observe industry reports, market tendencies, and competitor tactics. External factors affect the industry from the outside. Through the use of such tools as Political, Economic, Social, Technological, Environmental, and Legal (PESTEL) analysis, one can get a clear overview of the environment in which the industry survives.

Gather Customer Insights: Companies should conduct surveys and focus groups and use feedback now and then to understand customers' shifts in needs, desires, and challenges. This proactive stance enables organizations to anticipate market fluctuations and correspondingly modify their goods or services.

On the other hand, given continuous changes that occur in the business arena, adaptation becomes a prerequisite, and during these times, the vendor paradigm plays a significant role in formulating the vendor management strategy. Here are some strategic steps companies can undertake to maintain their competitive edge:

Utilize Strength, Weaknesses, Opportunities, and Threats (SWOT) Analysis: Conduct a SWOT Analysis regularly to examine the firm's internal capabilities and external environment critically. Sustainability, as a strategic tool, informs decision-making and, thus, prepares the company to make changes if needed.

Engage With Emerging Technologies: Firms should be ingrained in emerging technologies to remain competitive. This can be done by attending tech expos and conferences where one garners knowledge from new trends, networking with experts in this field, working together with technology start-ups and research institutions for co-innovation, investing in research and development, and innovation labs to develop relevant new technologies, encouraging teams to try out these technologies in small projects. Such programs not only improve technological capabilities but also promote a culture of innovation.

Leverage Data Analytics: In today's Big Data era, analytics are crucial in making informed decisions and adapting to market changes. Companies rely on various forms of analytics, such as predictive analytics to forecast future trends and customer behavior, real-time analytics for swift decision-making, and intuitive data visualizations to enhance understanding and decision-making processes. By embracing these practices and fostering a data-driven culture, organizations prioritize analytics over intuition, ensuring that decisions are grounded in data and insights rather than guesswork.

Encourage Open Communication: Such an environment allows collaboration and innovation. It can be achieved by establishing regular forums and check-ins where employees can discuss the implications of market/technology changes, encouraging cross-departmental collaboration for a broad perspective on possible changes, and creating psychological safety so that employees feel safe suggesting ideas and concerns with no reprimand.

In this dynamic world surrounded by changing technological and market situations, proactive adaptation becomes necessary. Here are the steps businesses can take to adapt proactively:

Anticipate Changes and Trends: Anticipate shifts before they are popularized.

Mitigate risks: Anticipate, detect, and anticipate likely challenges and plan strategies to reverse them before they impact the business.

Drive Innovation: Build a sense of a friendly environment that innovates, explores new technologies, and invents breakthrough products and services.

Enhance Agility: Develop the capability of quickly and effectively adjusting to market changes and changing consumer preferences.

Cultivate a Resilient Workforce: Make adaptability a part of the corporate culture, which results in a workforce that is ready for change and dynamic and flexible.

Secure Long-Term Success: Although reactive strategies offer immediate relief, proactive adaptation ensures survival and perpetuity.

Build Consumer Trust and Loyalty: Develop an image as an industry visionary focused on their regard for innovation and customer interests. You need to yearn to strengthen consumers' relationships.

Maximize Resource Efficiency: By strategically using resources and not ordering community resources in more quantity than you need, invest your community resources prudently to ensure that they match an organization's current and future trends and strategic endeavors.

Adopting changes isn't just a means to adapt to changes; it instead distinguishes a leader from a follower. It concerns leadership mainly based on anticipating others, being the first to react to the changes in the market, and achieving growth with the changes in the external environment.

Building a Culture of Innovation

The change is dynamic and fast-paced; technology has made the world a global village. It is a culture that encourages creativity, promotes originality, and supports innovative thinking (Sacolick, 2017). Here are the key elements that characterize an innovative culture:

- Leadership Commitment

Innovative cultures tend to be leadership-driven. Leaders must talk about innovation and evidence it in all their actions and decisions. They should establish a vision for innovation, spend resources, and participate personally in innovative initiatives.

- Openness to Ideas

It is most important to create a culture where ideas are shared regardless of department and hierarchy. All members of the organization should be ready to express opinions and recommendations without hesitation and uncertainty that they will never receive criticism.

- Tolerance for Failure

Innovation is about taking risks, not all of which work out. Failure should not be frowned upon in an innovative culture; instead, it is a learning and growing risk worth taking. It is all about celebrating the "fail fast, learn fast."

- Cross-functional Collaboration

Cross-functional teams promote innovation by harnessing various skills, perspectives, and spheres of expertise. Overcoming the silos and promoting cross-departmental collaboration may result in more holistic, inventive responses.

- Continuous Learning and Skill Development

An organization's employees should have updated skills and knowledge in order to innovate constantly. Training, professional development, and learning must be invested in to maintain the innovative culture.

- Agile and Flexible Processes

Rigid processes can stifle innovation. Agile methodologies and agility in project management enable timely changes, iterative development, and rapid reaction to feedback—all of which are necessary for innovation.

- Customer-Centric Approach

Innovations should finally cater to the customer. A culture that understands customer needs gathers feedback, and incorporates customers' insights into the innovation process is more likely to thrive.

- Recognition and Rewards

Identifying and rewarding innovative initiatives and results can contribute to the establishment of an innovation culture. Therefore, it is necessary to acknowledge the efforts, celebrate successes and bold attempts, and even learn from such failures.

- Resource Availability

Innovation requires investment. Regardless of the resources, time, money, or both required for experimenting, testing, and implementing ideas in teams is essential.

- A Supportive Environment:

The last piece is psychological safety—a culture where people feel safe, respected, and appreciated. Such an environment motivates team members to be risk-takers and think creatively.

Case Studies of Successful Technological Adaptations

The case studies reveal how organizations can handle technological disruption and use it to their advantage. Here are some noteworthy examples:

Netflix's Shift from DVDs to Streaming (BBC, 2018):

Such a case of successful technological adaptation is Netflix, which adapted it first as a DVD rental service and then grew to become a streaming monster. Here's a more detailed look at this transformation:

Background: The Inception and DVD Era.

Initial Model: In 1997, Netflix started as a DVD rental service. For its time, the model was innovative since it allowed for a subscription-based mail order to rent without paying late fees—an unprecedented deviation from what had been regarded as standard video rental stores.

Market Presence: First, Netflix's DVD rental service developed rapidly since people had their DVD players and wanted a better way to order.

Adaptation: Pivoting to Streaming.

Recognizing the Shift: With the rise of quicker Internet speeds and increased broadband penetration rates, Netflix's leadership saw an opportunity in online streaming. The company understood that with digital distribution, it could access unmatched convenience and a more extensive content library than regular DVDs.

Investing in Technology: Netflix initiated a vast project to build a robust streaming platform. This demanded huge investments into IT infrastructure, data centers, and content delivery networks to provide the best viewing quality without hitches.

Content Strategy Shift: At the same time, Netflix purchased and produced its work. This was a deliberate move to provide unique content and minimize the use of external providers.

Developing Personalization Algorithms: One of the major ingredients in Netflix's strategy was data analytics and machine learning, which enabled it to provide customized content recommendations. By analyzing viewing patterns, preferences, and behavior, Netflix was able to create recommendations based on users' engagement.

Outcome: Establishing Streaming Dominance.

Market Leadership: Netflix became a world leader in this arena as the shift to streaming took place. It challenged established television and film distribution systems, establishing a new benchmark for on-demand viewing.

Global Expansion and Content Library: The platform allowed Netflix to quickly globalize left, right, and center through its streaming service. The firm was also majorly investing in diversification of the content, such as international and locally produced shows and movies designed for diverse scope tastes and languages.

Adobe's Transition to a Subscription Model (Moorman, n.d.):

In the ensuing sections, we tackle a case study that illustrates how companies can effectively transform in light of technological disruptions and relevant market changes through Adobe's transition from perpetual licensing to a subscription model with the introduction of Creative Cloud. Here's a more detailed exploration:

Background: The Era of Licensed Software.

Traditional Model: In the following years, Adobe maintained its dominance as a software purveyor with proprietary products such as Photoshop, Illustrator, and Indesign. They were sold as individual units or packaged suites for considerable one-time fees.

Challenges: Adobe was the market leader, but it had severe problems. Its software was prohibitively costly, and the large-scale piracy that resulted heightened customer dissatisfaction with its infrequent release cycle of significant updates.

Adaptation: Shifting to Adobe Creative Cloud.

Strategic Decision: Taking advantage of the capabilities offered by cloud computing, preventing piracy, and easing software sharing, Adobe decided quickly enough to drastically change from a traditional licensing model to a subscription one.

Development of Adobe Creative Cloud: Adobe invested efforts in designing a coherent cloud computing environment featuring not only its well-known main products but also additional sets of tools and an array of services together with storage in the cloud. This platform made updating, collaboration, and mobility very easy.

Customer-Centric Features: The subscription model enabled Adobe to introduce regular updates and new features without waiting until significant releases. It also allows users to subscribe depending on their needs, making it possible for freelancers, home office workers, or small businesses.

Microsoft's Embrace of Cloud Computing (Day, 2016):

The strategic turn toward cloud computing is a turning point in the evolution of Microsoft, making it from a software-focused to a service-based company. This transition rejuvenated Microsoft's growth path and made it the leader of the cloud computing arena. Here's a deeper dive into this transformative journey:

Background: Navigating Market Shifts.

Initial Challenges: In the beginning, revenue from Microsoft primarily came from software sales—its Windows operating system and Office productivity suite. However, the advent of cloud computing, mobile devices, and consumer trends created enormous challenges for this business model.

Industry Disruption: The SaaS, PaaS, and IAAS models adopted by the IT industry spelled disaster for traditional software companies. The popularity of mobile devices and the growth in app usage diluted desktop-based computing.

Adaptation: Pivoting to Cloud Computing.

Strategic Realignment Under New Leadership: By appointing Satya Nadella as CEO in 2014, Microsoft confirmed its dedication to the cloud and innovation. Seizing the opportunity inside the cloud, Nadella turned this company from "a PC on every desk" to mobile-first and cloud-first.

Development of Azure: Microsoft heavily invested in creating Azure, its cloud computing technology, which integrates IaaS, PaaS, and SaaS, among other services. Azure was mainly developed to enable companies to build, deploy, and manage their applications and services via Microsoft-managed data centers.

Reorientation of Product Offerings: Microsoft changed its flagship product, the Office suite of programs, into cloud-based services with Office 365 (later renamed Microsoft 365). This transition gave users a consistent experience across devices, regular updates, and new collaboration apps.

BMW's Integration of IoT in Manufacturing (*An Insight into BMW Supply Chain Strategy: A Perfect Guide - 2023*, 2023):

BMW's deployment of IoT integration in its manufacturing is a modern concept demonstrating how to use technology for greater efficiency, quality, and creativity. Here's an in-depth look at this transformative initiative:

Background: A Commitment to Quality Manufacturing.

Prestigious Legacy: BMW is a market leader in the luxury automobile industry, with its reputation for quality, innovation, and engineering standards dating back several years. Sustaining and elevating this image involves systematic progress in manufacturing procedures.

Operational Efficiency and Quality: Like other manufacturers, BMW has had problems with operational efficiency, equipment maintenance, and quality control before integrating IoT. Improving these lags was essential to remain competitive and fulfill the rising demands of its clientele.

Adaptation: Embracing IoT in Operations.

Integration of IoT Technologies: BMW took a forward-thinking approach by incorporating IoT technologies into its manufacturing processes. This included deploying sensors and smart devices throughout its production plants to capture real-time data from equipment and machinery.

Data Analytics and Insights: The collected IoT data was used to explore the different areas of the manufacturing process. This helped BMW to track production in real time, identify potential threats, and act based on available information.

Predictive Maintenance: Predictive maintenance was a major IoT implementation. With equipment data analysis, BMW could forecast when a machine might need maintenance or repair, avoiding unnecessary downtime.

Streamlining Production Processes: The IoT allowed for more precise control and optimization of production processes. By providing real-time data, quick amendments were possible, increasing efficiency and eliminating waste.

Outcome: Capturing the value of Technological Innovation:

Domino's Transformation into a Tech Company (Kelso, n.d.):

Domino's emergence as a tech-oriented organization is an incredible example for all brands adapting to technology and how to adopt, change, and transform into something else. Let's delve deeper into this success story:

Background: Major Revival.

Declining Sales and Image Issues: Before its transformation, Domino's faced many challenges, such as waning sales performance, negative customer responses, and poor brand image. However, the older concept of phone-based orders and generic delivery systems no longer appealed to customers seeking convenience and quality.

Industry Evolution: The fast-food industry was changing rapidly, with technology becoming a leading component with which customers interacted with brands. Customer expectations for online ordering, delivery tracking, and digital payment were becoming common.

Adaptation: Embracing Technology at the Core.

Rebranding as a Tech Company: Domino's strategically shifted towards rebranding itself as a tech firm that sells pizza. This transformation called for a total revamp of its operating model, aiming at technology as the engine driving customer service and business growth.

Online Ordering and Delivery Tracking: Domino's spent a lot of money building order-making software that allows customers to easily place their orders. The software has more interactive features, such as ordering through the website, mobile app, and even social media platforms. Implementation of the Pizza Tracker enabled customers to trace their orders in real time, improving transparency and involvement.

AI-Driven Customer Service: Domino's incorporated AI into its customer service operations. Customer service has been transformed by the introduction of chatbots and virtual assistants such as "Dom," which offers instant, automated answers to questions while making order placement smooth.

Innovative Delivery Solutions: Domino's participated in cutting-edge delivery methods such as autonomous vehicles and drones, thus positioning it ahead of competitors.

Outcome: Realizing the industry leadership through technology innovation.

Conclusion

In wrapping up this chapter, it's clear that adapting to technological changes means more than just surviving – it's about shaping the future. Building an innovative culture and constantly evolving business strategies are key to staying ahead in today's ever-changing tech landscape. The strategies outlined in this chapter serve as a roadmap, urging organizations not just to react to change but to lead it. By turning disruptions into opportunities for innovation, businesses can ensure long-term sustainability. The essential tools for navigating this journey are foresight, agility, and a solid commitment to innovation – crucial for thriving in a technological upheaval.

Chapter 7: The Human Element in a Tech-Driven World

In today's tech-driven world, machines play a significant role in shaping industries and interactions, but human connection remains vital. This chapter explores how technology impacts human emotions, relationships, and awareness in a digital environment filled with AI algorithms, avatars, and virtual interactions.

We examine how technology affects mental health, balancing its benefits with potential drawbacks like overload and burnout. We explore how virtual teams across the globe navigate workplace dynamics, where algorithms make decisions alongside us.

Throughout this chapter, we aim to find ways to leverage technology while preserving human values. We consider integrating human behavior with technology to create positive work environments.

Ultimately, we envision a future where technology enhances rather than diminishes human experiences. Despite rapid digital progress, the human element remains central and evolving.

Mental Health and Remote Work

The emergence of remote work, primarily driven by global developments like the COVID-19 pandemic, has introduced a new era in professional lives. However, despite providing flexibility and reducing travel times, remote work may carry challenges specific to mental health. Let's examine the multifaceted mental health impacts of remote work:

Increased Flexibility and Autonomy

The switch to virtual work has redefined the standard working schedule, providing an element of convenience and independence once unachievable. Here's a more detailed look at its positive aspects and challenges:

Positive Aspects

Work-Life Balance: By practicing remote work, employees can align their working days with personal obligations and establish a more balanced relationship between professional and private life.

Reduced Commute Stress: Reducing daily commutes will save time and reduce stress, which will increase well-being, as more time can be devoted to private activities or rest.

Empowerment and Trust: Empowerment and trust develop with control of the work schedule. The workers who feel trusted that they can manage their time better are usually more motivated and happier with the job.

Challenges

Overworking Tendencies: The lack of a formal office setting implies that it is hard to turn off work. Working just a few feet away allows one to work longer hours, not leaving enough personal time and eventually contributing to burnout.

Boundary Setting: Separating work and home is difficult because both occur in the same location. Without such boundaries, work commitments tend to infringe on personal space, eroding healthy relationships and a healthy life.

Isolation and Lack of Social Interaction: One significant disadvantage associated with working from remote locations is reduced interaction, which may result in feelings of loneliness and dislocation. Here's a deeper insight into this challenge and strategies to mitigate it:

Challenges

Loss of Informal Communication: Water cooler talk and spontaneous meetings, which usually promote bonding and collaboration opportunities, don't occur when workers are at remote locations.
Professional Isolation: Sometimes, working remotely can make people feel left out or disconnected from the daily operations of a team, which indicates that they may experience loneliness and frustration.

Mitigation Strategies

Regular Virtual Check-Ins: Regular video conferences for reporting, ideation sessions, or even friendly chats may keep the teamwork going.

Online Social Events: Scrunching virtual social events like team lunches, happy hours, or interest-based clubs will allow employees to network and mingle alongside their work goals.

Digital Communication Platforms: Using programs such as Slack, Microsoft Teams, or Zoom for daily communication can ensure there is a constant flow of conversation and interaction so that team members maintain their connections and support.

Communication and Collaboration Difficulties

Transitioning to remote work has already changed how people communicate and collaborate, giving rise to new challenges that could influence team dynamics and project results. Here's an in-depth look at these challenges and strategies to mitigate them:

Challenges

Inconsistent Communication: Remote working may result in delayed or inconsistent communication, leading to clarity and smooth work progress. Different time zones or work schedules may make team members feel disconnected.

Loss of Nonverbal Cues: The lack of nonverbal components in remote communication can lead to misunderstandings or a lack of emotional connection during interactions.

Exclusion of Remote Team Members: With a hybrid team, some members are in the office and others remote, which could lead to segregation of 'in'-group and 'out'- groups, resulting in exclusion feelings for those who remain working from home.

Mitigation Strategies

Establish Clear Communication Protocols: Draw clear communication channels and procedures for different forms of communication (for instance, instant messaging vs. Ensure that video calls (among other protocols) are enforced and understood by all team members.

Regular and Structured Check-Ins: Conducting check-ins or standup meetings on a routine will ensure that everyone is clear about the current project's status, pending tasks, and what needs urgent action.

Leverage Collaboration Tools: Use collaborative tools and platforms that provide real-time communication, document sharing, and project management features to ensure everyone on the team can access relevant information.

Inclusive Meeting Practices: To facilitate equitable participation for remote team members in hybrid teams, provide equal chances to contribute during meetings. Employ technology so that every participant can see and hear each other clearly, as well as participation from all team members.

Home Environment Challenges

Remote work transition has brought the home environment into an active position of work relations, which can produce new challenges that might determine individual productivity and welfare. Here are the challenges and strategies for addressing them:

Challenges

Inadequate Workspaces: A workstation is only available to some at home, which can result in pain or loss of productivity.

Distractions and Interruptions: A home setting can be full of distractions, for instance, manipulating household chores or the presence of family members and pets that might distract focus.

Overlapping of Personal and Professional Life: Being physically distant is not to "work" and "home" space can create challenges in setting boundaries, interfering with relaxation time.

Mitigation Strategies

Home Office Stipends or Reimbursements: Provide financial support for workers to create ergonomic and time-saving home offices. This may include allowances for ergonomic chairs, desks, or IT equipment.

Guidelines for Creating Productive Workspaces: Share tips and best practices with employees for setting up a home office, dealing with the distractions that working from home presents, etc.

Respect for Work-Life Boundaries: Encourage a culture that values individual time and privacy. Incentivize employees to keep regular office hours and fully detach from work outside of working time.

Mental Health and Well-Being Resources: Provide resources like online counseling, wellness sessions, or mental health days that help employees cope with the issue of remote work and its related challenges.

Impact On Work-Life Balance

The shift toward telecommuting has changed the work-life balance of many professionals. Flexibility is offered, but it creates challenges that can muddle the lines drawn between professional responsibilities and private life. Here's a closer look at the challenges and strategies for mitigating them:

Challenges

Overextension and Burnout: The ease of having a workplace at home makes people devote more hours to work, as the boundaries between work time and personal time are unclear. However, this overstretch may result in burnout and impaired mental health.

Difficulty Switching Off: Isolation from an office, where one would physically disconnect and return home to mentally switch off work activities, is no longer possible.

Mitigation Strategies

Defined Work Hours and Breaks: Press the employees to create and maintain certain work hours and have proper rest breaks in between. This guarantees that work time remains separate from personal life.

Promoting Physical and Mental Well-Being: Create programs encouraging physical activities, mindfulness practices, and hobbies. This helps ensure the employee maintains a balance between work and other activities.

Time Management Training: Providing training on good time management can help employees plan their activities effectively and manage their workload, thereby preventing many perils related to overworking.

Leadership by Example: Managers and leaders should emulate healthy work-life balance practices to encourage outcomes when observed by employees.

Access to Support and Resources

Although working remotely offers an opportunity to reach out for more support and resources, maintaining connections with employees becomes challenging. Here's an exploration of the positive aspects and challenges, along with strategies to address them:

Positive Aspect

Flexible Access to Support: Employees may access a wide range of support resources remotely, such as online counseling services, digital wellness platforms, and virtual communities. This flexibility is especially adequate for those seeking confidential and fast mental health care.

Challenges

The feeling of Disconnection from Support Systems: Remote employees may miss the support structures that a physical office provides, including HR representatives, peer groups, and informal chats among co-workers.

Underutilization of Resources: Employees who telecommute may need to learn about or adequately use their support resources because they require more information and time to access such services.

Mitigation Strategies

Regular Communication of Available Resources: Ensure that every employee is aware of the support resources and how to access them easily.

Virtual Support Groups and Events: Organize virtual support groups or hold online events focusing on mental well-being, stress management, and healthy approaches to work. These programs can create a sense of belonging and enable people to share their experiences and advise on how best to deal with such fears.

Proactive Check-Ins by HR and Managers: Encourage regular check-ins between HR personnel and managers, providing a platform for them to discuss issues that could be facing the remote employee while offering feedback and guiding employees towards relevant support resources.

Workplace well-being, especially in remote or tech environments, is paramount as it helps the workers to stay healthy and productive. Here are several strategies that organizations and individuals can employ to enhance well-being:

Promote Physical Health

Encourage Regular Exercise: Incentivize employees to pursue physical activities through fitness challenges or corporate gym memberships and provide them with stipends for home exercise equipment.

Ergonomic Workspaces: Offer advice and assistance in creating ergonomic home offices to avoid workplace discomfort.

Support Mental and Emotional Health

Access to Mental Health Resources: Offer mental health services by integrating employee assistance programs (EAPs) or collaborations with the Mental Health Platform.

Mindfulness and Stress Management Programs: Provide programs or workshops on mindfulness, meditation, and stress management that will enable employees to find mechanisms for dealing with the pressure.

Foster Social Connections

Virtual Social Events: Arrange virtual social events, team-building activities, or interest groups to establish a feeling of belonging in remote workers.

Mentorship and Peer Support Programs: Initiate mentorship or peer support programs to distribute information, provide advice, and fulfill mental needs.

Cultivate a Positive Work Culture

Recognition and Appreciation: Establish recognition programs that recognize employees' achievements, milestones, and contributions to increase their morale.

Open Communication Channels: Keep the lines open where employees feel secure. Feedback sessions, town halls, or anonymous surveys can be used to gather insights and address concerns.

Promote Work-Life Balance

Respect Boundaries: Learn about work-life boundaries, discourage after-work communications, and motivate workers to use "do not disturb" features at the workplace.

Flexible Work Arrangements: Provide employees with flexible work hours or compressed working weeks so that they can balance their professional and personal obligations in an efficient way.

Encourage Professional Growth

Learning and Development Opportunities: Offer learning opportunities that help with ongoing education and career advancement, such as access to online courses or workshops.

Career Pathing and Progression: Provide clear career paths and development opportunities so employees can see a future ahead in the organization.

Regular Check-Ins and Support

Proactive Wellness Check-Ins: Ensure well-being, workload, and support conversations are part of standard job processing.

Leadership Support and Role Modeling: Promote health-work habits among leaders and managers by encouraging them to engage in wellness activities that emphasize their importance.

Fostering Human Connections in a Digital World

Significant Communication in a Digitalized World

In a digital setting, communication is subtly different. It is also essential to focus on meaningful communication to maintain relationships, promote cooperation, and ensure that everyone in the team feels valued. Here's a guide to help you prioritize meaningful communication in your organization:

Encourage Video Calls

Set Expectations: Provide specific instructions on when to utilize video calls instead of the other communication tools. Foster video calls in team meetings, one-on-ones, or when discussing complicated issues that work better physically.

Create a Comfortable Environment: Make sure that team members have a quiet work area for video calls. Promote the use of cameras to create a more intimate conversation.

Be Mindful of Video Call Fatigue: Strike between video conferencing and respecting people's time and attention. Keep meetings short and on topic to avoid boredom.

Promote Active Listening

Practice Attentive Listening: In a virtual meeting, fully listen to the speaker as doing something else simultaneously and not giving visual cues like nodding or smiling shows disinterest.

Encourage Participation: Make sure every team member is comfortable voicing their opinions. Allow people to respond freely and give everyone an opportunity.

Summarize and Reflect: After discussions, summarize them and reflect on what you heard to clarify whether the speaker was understood properly.

Social Hours and Virtual Events

Regularly Schedule Social Time: Establish a routine for virtual social gatherings such as happy hours or coffee breaks where employees engage without discussing work.

Plan Engaging Activities: Structuring virtual events like team-building activities, trivia games, or talent shows can keep these social hours entertaining.

Be Inclusive in Planning: Share the function of organizing social hours among teammates and be prepared for different activities to meet various interests or cultures.

Interest-Based Groups

Identify Common Interests: Conduct a poll to determine what activities or interests the team members share. The information can be used to form groups or clubs around these interests.

Provide a Platform for Interaction: Set up specific areas for these interest groups using platforms such as Slack, Microsoft Teams, or Facebook Groups.

Support and Encourage Participation: Incentivize leaders and managers to adopt such initiatives by joining them and appreciating the significance of these groups in building a sense of community.

Culture of Empathy and Support

Cultivating an empathetic and supportive culture not only leads to a happier employee base but also helps build more forthcoming and creative teams. Here's a guide on how to foster such a culture:

Emotional Intelligence Training

Implement Comprehensive Training Programs: Provide workshops or training programs that aim to increase emotional intelligence, such as self-awareness, self-regulation, and motivation.

Integrate EI Into Daily Operations: Promote emotional intelligence principles in leadership styles and day-to-day work for managers and team leaders.

Promote Continuous Learning: Create materials for the continuous development of emotional intelligence, such as articles, literature works, books, podcasts, or online courses.

Establish Support Networks

Create Peer Mentoring Programs: Partner employees with mentors who offer advice, assistance, and feedback to enable them to overcome the challenges of working in an environment and develop personally.

Form Support Groups: Create groups where individuals can talk about their workplace difficulties, challenges with work-life balance, or anything else in a safe and supportive environment.

Encourage Open Dialogue: Set up forums where individuals dialogue about their work and share what deterred them and how they overcame challenges to realize successes. This may involve regular team meetings, virtual coffee chats, or anonymous feedback tools.

Encouraging Collaboration and Teamwork

The foundation of a vibrant and active working place is collaboration and teamwork. Here's how to encourage and facilitate effective collaboration:

Utilize Collaborative Tools and Platforms

Select the Right Tools: Select collaborative technologies that fit your team's requirements in communication (such as Slack or Microsoft Teams), project management (like Asana and Trello), or document sharing (Google Docs and SharePoint).

Train Your Team: Make sure that everyone on your team is well-trained and relaxed with the tools you are using. Keep them updated on new features or tips to make the processes easier.

Encourage Active Participation: Make these platforms a culture whereby every team member can contribute, share ideas, and provide feedback.

Engage Teams in Collaborative Projects and Goals

Set Clear Collective Goals: Set concrete, attainable goals for team projects, ensuring each member knows they are a part of the project and what it entails.

Foster an Environment of Co-Creation: Encourage teammates to engage in brainstorming and co-creating solutions. This not only yields better results but also makes everyone feel as if they own the result.

Celebrate Team Achievements: Praise the group as a whole rather than just individual members. This also underscores the importance of working as a team and coordinated action.

Implement Inclusive Practices

Inclusive Communication

Cultural Sensitivity: Appreciate cultural differences in communication. Train employees on cultural awareness to avoid misinterpretations and possible offenses.

Language Considerations: For global teams, offer or translate essential communications in several languages. Use simple language to ensure that messages are clear.

Inclusive Content: Ensure that all communications, internal or external, reflect diversity and do not marginalize any group. Choose examples, images, and scenarios that represent a cross-section of people or situations.

Accessibility of Digital Tools

Assess Tool Accessibility: Assess the accessibility features of digital tools, as they should be usable by people with disabilities. This also encompasses compatibility with screen readers, captioning features on videos, and mouse alternative keyboard navigation.

Employee Training on Accessibility Features: Train your employees on the use of accessibility functions in digital tools. Train employees about the essentiality of these features and how they promote inclusion.

Solicit Feedback on Tool Use: Ask employees for feedback about digital tools being used regularly. Ensure there is a mechanism for handling any case related to accessibility.

Promote Transparency and Openness

Regular Updates and Check-Ins

Consistent Communication: Set up a consistent communications schedule with leadership to give regular updates about changes in company news, project progress, or any alteration. This fosters a culture of transparency where employees feel informed and engaged.

Open Forums for Discussion: Employees can express their ideas and feedback. This can be achieved by holding regular town hall meetings, Q&A sessions with leaders, or even a digital suggestion box.

Check-Ins for Personal Connection: Prompt the managers to engage in constant one-on-one interactions with their team members apart from talking about work matters and help them identify problems depriving them of that personal connection.

Leadership Accessibility

Open Door Policy: Encourage an open-door policy where employees can discuss their ideas, concerns, or feedback with leaders.

Leadership Presence in Digital Spaces: Make sure the leaders come to life on digital communication channels by replying to emails promptly, responding to online forum discussions, or participating virtually.

Mentorship and Support: Promote leaders to become mentors who give advice and care for employees' professional development and personal growth.

Balancing Automation with Employee Well-Being

On the one hand, adopting automated technologies provides opportunities for individuals to reap benefits for well-being. However, while automation can significantly increase efficiency, productivity, and the nature of work, that is dangerous for millions who might lose their jobs or the quality of human-machine interaction. Here's an exploration of the relationship between automation and well-being:

Positive Impacts of Automation on Well-Being

Reduction of Tedious and Repetitive Tasks

Humans are good at creative activities, strategic planning, and other essential things that automation cannot. This may result in high levels of contentment, a sense of meaning, and potential for career development.

Enhanced Work Safety

Automated systems help to eliminate mentally and physically unsafe tasks, eliminating the risk of workplace-related accidents or stress for employees.

Increased Productivity and Efficiency

Automation can simplify processes, minimize errors, and guarantee consistency in results, all of which create a more effective workplace whereby staff can complete more tasks simultaneously.

Opportunities for Skill Development and Career Growth

With the automation of routine tasks, workers have an opportunity to undertake upskilling or reskilling and shift across cognitive careers that require higher-order thinking and creativity functions, such as emotional intelligence.

Challenges and Considerations Regarding Automation and Well-being:

Job Displacement and Insecurity

One significant issue related to automation is job displacement. The fear of being fired can cause stress, anxiety, and insecurity among employees.

Skill Obsolescence and the Need for Reskilling

Technological advancements are happening phenomenally; thus, workers have no option but to develop new skills constantly. Pressure to keep up with the latest technologies can create stress and may involve a considerable investment in training.

Changes in Work Dynamics and Human Interaction

Automation can change working dynamics by reducing human contact or even changing collaboration and communication practices.

Monitoring and Privacy Concerns

Monitoring is a standard feature of automated systems that is beneficial for performance from an analytical and improvement perspective but can also be viewed as challenging individuals' personal lives or reaffirming the "big brother" feeling.

Strategies to Enhance Well-Being in the Context of Automation

Transparent Communication and Involvement

Raise employee concerns about automation initiatives and involve them in making decisions.

Support for Reskilling and Upskilling

Offer resources and training programs in new skills for employees to support their work transition due to automation.

Focus On Human-Centric Design

Develop automated systems that support human capabilities, thus ensuring that technology enriches rather than reduces the quality of performance and workplace relations.

Prioritize Mental Health and Support Services

Make mental health resources, counseling services, and support groups available to enable employees to cope with the changes that come with automation.

Ethical Considerations and Workforce Planning

To begin with, introduce ethical guidelines for automation so that the implementation of automated systems takes into account the influence on jobs welfare and general society.

A holistic approach to automation adoption that considers employee health includes a forward-looking strategy, diligent

preparation, and operations with morality in mind. Here are strategies that organizations can adopt to ensure a balanced approach:

Strategic Workforce Planning

Conduct detailed evaluations to determine which activities are best suited for automation and must remain human-led, considering aspects like value addition, complexity, and the involvement of human empathy and decision-making.

Plan for the future workforce by predicting the effects of automation on job roles and developing actions such as redeployment, reskilling, or upskilling if necessary.

Inclusive Decision-Making and Transparency

Make employees part of discussions on automation strategies and decisions to give them a voice and understand this process. Being honest about what one is trying to achieve by automating the expected outcomes and possible consequences helps minimize fear and uncertainty.

Investment in Reskilling and Upskilling

Offer thorough training materials for employees to understand how the role can work with new technologies. This will close the skills gap and show that this organization prioritizes its employees. Develop a lifelong learning culture that promotes constant professional development and personal growth.

Employee Well-Being and Support Systems

Provide support systems, such as counseling, mental health facilities, and stress management programs, to ease employees through the change process. Acknowledge and attend to the affective aspects of automation, ensuring that employees are considered humans rather than robots.

Ethical and Human-Centric Automation

Implement ethical standards concerning automation and AI use, ensuring that these two technologies are applied in a manner that benefits employees, customers, and society as a whole. Develop and deploy automation technologies that strengthen human capacities, increase work satisfaction, and improve the quality of jobs.

Promotion of Work-Life Balance

Automate tasks to mitigate workload and eliminate boredom among employees, freeing them up for more creative-led work. Protect work-life boundaries, ensuring new efficiency does not imply longer working hours or intrusion into personal life.

Regular Review and Adjustment

Periodically evaluate the impact of automation on workers and organizational goals. Recognize that you may need to change strategies based on feedback, performance information, and changing conditions. Cultivate an adaptive and resilient corporate culture that can adjust to the changing needs and demands of employees and customers.

Conclusion

In Chapter 7, "The Human Element in a Tech-Driven World," we delved into how technology impacts business efficiency and the well-being of individuals in the workplace.

We examined how remote work affects mental health. While it offers freedom, it also brings challenges like isolation and overwork. We discussed strategies like clear routines and communication to support well-being in remote settings.

We also explored how digital tools affect human connections. While they provide convenience, they can sometimes weaken face-to-face interactions. We suggested using virtual social spaces and fostering empathy to maintain strong human bonds.

Additionally, we addressed the challenges of automation, such as job security and human-machine interactions. We discussed approaches to balance automation with human well-being, emphasizing ethical implementation and continuous learning.

Overall, we emphasized the importance of considering the human element in a technology-driven world. We advocated for strategies that prioritize well-being, foster human connections, and integrate automation responsibly.

To wrap up this chapter, we underline the importance of the human factor in technocracy. The essence of taking advantage of technology depends on our understanding, appreciation, and fulfillment of the human aspect of change. By developing work environments that emphasize mental health and human connections and integrating automation into the well-being of employees, organizations will be able to build more productive and kinder, tough-going ones.

Chapter 8: Inclusive Work Environments

At the heart of today's organizational landscape lies a transformative idea reshaping the modern workplace: fostering inclusivity. This chapter illustrates workplaces evolving beyond traditional roles to become vibrant ecosystems where diversity and inclusion permeate the culture, strategy, and daily operations. It envisions an idealized business environment recognizing the strength and value of a diverse workforce with varied backgrounds and life experiences.

Throughout this chapter, we embark on an intriguing journey to unravel the concept of inclusive work environments and witness them in action. This journey challenges preconceived notions, uncovers profound insights, and inspires us to become agents of change. Here, we lay the groundwork for organizations that embrace and celebrate the rich tapestry of human diversity. Such environments are not just reflections of societal diversity; they are dynamic entities that thrive on and benefit from the diverse perspectives and talents within them. As we delve deeper into this discussion, we begin to envision future workplaces. In this place, diversity flourishes alongside opportunity and potential.

Diversity and Inclusion in the Future Workplace

Diversity and inclusion are poised to become a critical factor in shaping the future of work, moving from pure compliance or corporate social responsibility mandates into strategic imperatives. The future workplace will not take note of diversity and inclusivity but embrace them fully as enablers of innovation, engagement, and competition (Warren, 2022). Here's an exploration of diversity and inclusion in the future workplace:

Strategic Imperative

Over time, organizations will understand that the quality of commitment to diversity and inclusion is a significant competitive advantage differentiator and an internal innovation driver for business growth. This strategic imperative involves:

Integrating D&I in Business Strategy: Diversity and inclusion will be infused into the very nature of business strategies, guiding such crucial decisions as product development, marketing efforts, and customer service, all based on an understanding that is deeper than mere tolerance.

Leadership Commitment: The top executives will promote inclusion and diversity and be held responsible for ensuring that these values are integrated within the organization. This commitment is also evident in the allocation of resources, policy formulation, and prioritizing initiatives to support an inclusive working environment.

Data-Driven Decision Making: Relying on data, organizations set specific goals and monitor performance progress towards the established objectives to evaluate whether diversity and inclusion measures were effective. The data-driven approach provides transparency and accountability and emphasizes areas for improvement in the performance gap.

Holistic Approach to Diversity

The workplace of tomorrow will approach diversity from many angles, recognizing the complex shades that humanity wears. This holistic approach involves:

Recognizing Intersectionality means knowing that people can belong to several groups with various and diverse backgrounds whose overlapping identities affect their interactions with work.

Broadening Recruitment Strategies: Utilizing different recruitment channels and working with organizations that promote the interests of underrepresented groups.

Fostering a Diverse Talent Pipeline: Investment in education, mentorship, and development programs that foster talent among underrepresented groups, reflecting diversity on every level, from entry-level positions to senior positions.

Inclusion as a Cultural Norm

A culture-inclusive environment is not just a policy; it's an atmosphere where each individual feels welcomed and valued. This includes:

Inclusive Language and Communication: Respectful language and ensuring the organization's commitment to diversity and inclusion are reflected in internal and external communications.

Safe Spaces for Dialogue and Feedback: Enabling employees to have spaces where they can share their experiences and opinions, raise issues of concern, and proffer suggestions in a healthy environment.

Inclusive Benefits and Policies: Providing benefits, policies, and resources that are tailored for the workforce's specifically diverse needs, such as offering employees flexible working or different parental leave policies or alternative health and wellness programs depending on cultural tradition, lifestyle preferences, or particular strain status.

Technology and Inclusion

The growing importance of using technology to facilitate and promote diversity has emerged as a crucial element for organizations. This can be seen in:

Innovative Recruitment Tools: Using AI-based recruitment tools that ease unconscious bias in recruiting by emphasizing skills and qualifications instead of race, gender, etc.

Accessibility Features in Tech Tools: Digital tools can be made available to all employees, including those with disabilities, by having screen readers alongside subtitles or an alternative input method.

Virtual Collaboration Platforms: We are introducing platforms that promote collaboration and inclusion, where team members from different locations, physical limitations, or time zones can provide equal input to project decisions.

Addressing Unconscious Bias

The subtlety of unconscious bias can insidiously creep into decision-making and behaviors that may compromise diversity and inclusion efforts. Organizations are recognizing the importance of addressing this head-on.

Comprehensive Bias Training: Use of frequent, detailed training programs that help employees and leaders realize and understand their unconscious biases. These sessions are not just about awareness but also offer practical tools and techniques on how to address bias in determining justice.

Bias Audits in Processes: Frequently audit company processes, especially recruitment, promotion, and performance evaluation, to discover aspects that may unknowingly instill bias.

Encouraging Open Dialogue: Generating safe environments where employees can talk and mark cases of bias. This openness enables the identification of bias as a human characteristic that can be dealt with positively.

Empowerment Through Employee Resource Groups (ERGs)

ERGs are evolving as powerful platforms for driving inclusion and empowerment within organizations.

Resource Allocation for ERGs: Furnishing ERGs with the necessary resources, support, and executive sponsorship that should enable initiatives to have a tangible impact.

Integrating ERG Insights into Policies: Building policies on the insights of ERGs such that diverse views are considered in developing organizational strategies.

Celebrating ERG Contributions: Acknowledging and appreciating ERGs' efforts to promote a diverse and inclusive culture, reinforcing their worth to the corporation.

Measurement and Accountability

Tangible metrics and accountability structures are critical to driving real progress in diversity and inclusion.

Clear, Measurable Goals: Development of specific, tangible goals about diversity and inclusion metrics such as representation targets, retention rates, or employee satisfaction scores across minority groups.

Regular Reporting and Transparency: Reporting regularly on progress towards diversity and inclusivity goals, emphasizing openness, and building a culture of responsibility.

Linking Outcomes to Performance: Incorporating diversity and inclusion metrics into the broader leadership and team performance management systems with rewards for improvements in these areas.

Leadership Commitment and Role Modelling

The role of leaders in shaping and driving an inclusive culture is paramount.

Visible Commitment: Leaders act as visible and vocal champions of diversity initiatives, signaling their relevance to everyone in the organization.

Inclusive Leadership Training: Training leaders on inclusive practices that value empathy, listening skills, and cultural competence.

Walking the Talk: To ensure that the leaders advocate for diversity and inclusion and demonstrate these values in their day-to-day activities, decisions, and interactions.

Addressing Bias in Hiring and Advancement

Addressing bias in appointment and promotion is paramount to establishing a truly diverse and inclusive working environment where every employee has fair access to growth and success (Georghiou, n.d.). Increasingly, organizations are understanding the need to eliminate biases—both conscious and unconscious—in hiring practices and career progression.

Organizations are working hard to ensure fairness and efficiency in their hiring processes. To achieve this, they're adopting innovative practices like blind hiring. In blind hiring, resumes and applications are anonymized, meaning that information like a candidate's gender or ethnicity is removed. This allows organizations to focus solely on candidates' skills and qualifications, ensuring a fairer selection process. Blind hiring not only promotes fairness but also maximizes the use of talent in the applicant pool.

The formation of diverse hiring panels is essential to increase the objectivity of the hiring process even more. Team members from different lines of business, women, minorities, departments, and hierarchical levels combine to provide multiple points of view. This variety works to achieve some measure of neutrality and objectively assess the candidates.

But that's not enough to establish diverse panels. Bias awareness and training for human resources (HR) personnel and hiring managers are always necessary. Such training sessions should revolve around the various forms of biases and their effects on human judgment and prescribe practical methods for identifying and reducing undesirable biases.

Furthermore, mentorship and sponsorship are vital in helping to create the right working climate. Mentoring by competent, supportive mentors of employees from minority groups or leaders who promote their mentees drives change toward the increasing representation of minorities in leadership positions.

The key is also the creation of measurable, objective, and consistently enforced standards for promotions and career bracketing. To do so, organizations must be vigilant regarding promotion, incumbency, and potential patterns that might indicate biases and correct proffered recommendations, presumably strategically.

In the field of decision-making, as the move toward a data-driven approach induced this, it has indeed imprinted a substantial development to the frames of organizational development. From the recruitment and hiring process to even the promotion of an employee, organizations are utilizing data and analytics to make well-informed, strategic decisions. Artificial Intelligence-powered resume screening tools, performance information from successful employees, and balanced scorecards in performance evaluation are ways data drives objective, transparent, and equitable work environments.

The significance of collecting and processing employee responses is unequivocal. Periodic surveys, feedback negotiations, and sentiment analysis machinery provide priceless details concerning employee satisfaction, engagement, and general organizational culture. These arguments guide constant implementation initiatives and assist in identifying and solving any cultural and framework delivery issues.

Creating Accessible Work Environments

Making work environments accessible is a logical step in building an inclusive organizational culture that enables each person, irrespective of their physical and digital accessibility requirements, to perform successfully. Accessibility should be viewed as a persistent initiative that includes physical and digital environments.

Physical and digital accessibility are practically imperative when it comes to workspaces and office setups. Creating an inclusive environment implies that the provision would involve adjusting both physical working space and digital tools to accommodate a wide variety of needs.

Physical Accessibility

Workspace Design: Office space designs or retrofits should observe accessibility specifications. This is achieved through the provision of wheelchair-friendly entrances, corridors, work centers, and bathrooms. Additionally, offering adaptive furniture like adjustable desks and ergonomic chairs allows for meeting a range of physical needs, thus creating a flexible workspace capable of servicing an array of individuals.

Accessible Facilities: In addition to individual workplaces, accessibility refers to shared amenities. Meeting rooms, cafeterias, and recreational areas should be helpful for everybody, including ramps, lifts, or tactile marks to assist individuals with handicaps that impede mobility or vision. Furthermore, considering some acoustic and lighting aspects can improve conditions for those with auditory or visual sensitivities in the workspace.

Emergency Preparedness: A complete emergency evacuation plan must address the needs of employees and people with disabilities. Routine drills, properly designated escape paths, and readily available protection procedures ensure that safety is everybody's concern throughout the organization.

Digital Accessibility

Inclusive Technology and Tools: Digital tools, software, and platforms must be readily available and compatible with assistive technologies like screen readers, speech recognition apps, or alternative devices. Regular checks and updates are required to maintain compliance with standards such as the Web Content Accessibility Guidelines (WCAG) and facilitate accessibility.

Accessible Content: The digital content has to be formulated with disability in mind. This includes but is not limited to, the use of subtitles or transcripts for audio and video content, opting for alt-text for images, and making documents accessible when navigated through keyboard controls. Simplicity and a few words will be paired with content offered in different kinds of packages satisfying many different preferences.

Training and Support

Education on Digital Accessibility: By all employees, the meaning and realities of digital accessibility, both semantic and practical, are crucial. This involves training in accessible content design and the use of digital tools.

Technical Support: Providing exclusive and specialized tech support to help employees, especially those with disabilities, navigate and work effectively with online sources is a top illustration of an organization that supports inclusiveness.

Conceiving an equitable workplace is a continuous evolution toward the work environment that calls for consistent use of feedback, continuous improvement, and a passion for recognizing what kind of talents are in the people and the proper utility. This undertaking goes beyond simple adherence to the regulatory standards. Still, it is an ambitious undertaking that seeks to foster an environment whereby every person, regardless of their limitations, can succeed.

Feedback and Continuous Improvement

The process of feedback and continuous improvement plays a critical role. Employees must be encouraged to contribute their own views of the actual and digital places within the organization. Given the efforts to become aware of it, positive feedback actively seeks and values this feedback, allowing working on concrete improvement of the workspace that corresponds to the identified needs and challenges. Building a continual process of reviews and improvements for accessibility is a must. This is more than just a description of refinement; it implies that inclusivity is also integrated into the organization's culture.

Proactive Recruitment and Hiring

Right from the stage of recruitment, the journey towards inclusivity starts. The basic intervention is to adopt reactive recruitment strategies targeting individuals with disabilities. This requires working with agencies that foster the employment of people with disabilities and posting job advertisements that promote inclusivity. Making sure that the recruitment process is open to every candidate is critical. This could also mean offering the application documents in different forms, having the signing interpreters, or ensuring that interviewing places are accessible.

Customized Onboarding and Orientation

Upon arrival, targeted onboarding and orientation programs uniquely adjusted to meet the needs of employees with disabilities have a vital role to play. These initiatives need to provide materials in friendly alternative formats and should hold inclusive orientation days. Allowing a new hire to get a buddy or a mentor would give them the necessary guidance, hence easing integration into the workplace culture.

Workplace Modifications and Accommodations

Acknowledging that everyone is different is one of the factors needed to create such an environment. This acknowledgment materializes thus in the form of suitable accommodations, such as space re-designs, flexible schedules, specialized equipment, or adaptive software. Dialogue that continues over time with employees to understand and respond to changing needs keeps the workplace a comfortable space for everyone.

Inclusive Communication and Collaboration

It is costly to sell a communication culture that is aware of differences. Disability awareness and communication training also equip employees with the knowledge of interacting with customers with compassion.

Fostering an Inclusive Culture

Develop a culture that appreciates diversity and inclusiveness. This involves promoting diversity, developing empathy and understanding, and discouraging discrimination or bias.

Create employee resource groups (ERGs) or support networks that allow employees of varying abilities to meet, share their stories, and lobby for adopting inclusive practices.

Feedback and continuous improvement

Frequently get feedback from employees about workplace inclusivity. This feedback should guide continuous work to enhance policies, practices, and the working atmosphere.

Ensure that leadership supports and actively contributes to promoting inclusivity as an organizational model, driving ongoing improvement.

Conclusion

Throughout our journey, we've learned that inclusion and diversity go beyond having different people around. They're about creating cultures where everyone feels valued, and every idea is respected. We've seen how important it is to break biases in hiring, promotions, and daily interactions and to make fair decisions with transparency.

We've also explored the importance of accessibility, understanding that true inclusion means making all parts of the workplace accessible, both physically and digitally, so that everyone can contribute.

In conclusion, creating more inclusive workplaces is an ongoing effort that requires consistent commitment and action. It's a journey toward a workplace that fosters innovation and success and reflects our values of supporting diversity, dynamism, and inclusivity in society.

This chapter serves as a guidepost for the future, showing us how diversity, inclusion, and accessibility can be integrated into organizational culture. In this future economy, businesses will thrive financially by embracing the diversity and equity of their human capital. Let's use this guidance as we move forward and build workplaces that are efficient and truly human in every sense.

Chapter 9: Government Policies in the Future of Work

Throughout this journey, we aim to highlight the importance of government policies in responding to and shaping changes in work dynamics. This chapter emphasizes the need for proactive government action and collaboration among policymakers, business leaders, and the workforce. Such collaboration is essential for creating an innovative, dynamic, and inclusive future, considering the widespread benefits of technological advancement. However, it also unveils a narrative where government decisions and actions influence future workplaces, showcasing the intertwined relationship between politics and progress.

Social Safety Nets in the Gig Economy

The rise of the gig economy has reshaped the nature of work, offering workers newfound freedom but also introducing unique challenges (Watt & Australia. Parliament. Senate. Select Committee on The Future Of Work And Workers, 2018). Governments worldwide are implementing policies to ensure fair treatment and adequate benefits for gig workers. These interventions seek to level the playing field and address the specific challenges faced by individuals in the gig economy.

Classification and Rights of Gig Workers

Both the categorization and rights of gig workers need a sophisticated perspective on the contemporary labor force and personalized rules grounded in the realities of gig work. Here's a more profound exploration:

Clarifying Worker Status

Legislative Frameworks: Governments are crafting comprehensive legislative frameworks to clarify the status of gig workers. These frameworks delineate distinctions between traditional employees, independent contractors, and gig workers. They consider factors such as the degree of work control, flexibility in working hours, and access to necessary tools.

Legal Precedents and Guidelines: By setting precedents, judicial decisions and legal guidelines are influencing the classification of gig economy workers to an ever-increasing extent.

Ensuring Basic Worker Rights

Minimum Wage and Fair Compensation: Introducing and adopting policies that ensure gig workers earn reasonable pay for their work following local minimum wage laws when applicable, as well as proper payment models based on the actual time spent at a given job.

Protection Against Unlawful Termination: Develop regulations that safeguard gig workers from sudden or misplaced termination and provide an adequate platform for addressing grievances and complaints.

Social Security and Benefits

As the gig economy continues to thrive, there is an increasing need for social security and benefits that can address the distinct aspect of gig work. Here's how policies are evolving in this domain:

Access to Social Benefits

Inclusion in Social Security Schemes: Expanding social security benefits to gig workers, either by including them in existing programs or developing specialized schemes geared toward the character of freelance work.

Health Insurance Options: Offering health insurance plans to gig workers, including government-gig platforms in collaboration with insurers that offer tailored coverages based on user needs and affordability.

Portable Benefits Systems

Designing Portable Benefits: Creating benefits systems that are not employer-oriented but attached to the worker. With these systems, benefits accumulate and are portable across the jobs or platforms that gig workers switch between.

Contribution-Based Models: We are building models in which contributions towards benefits can be made by gig workers, gig platforms, and potentially the government so that the worker would have retirement savings, an instance of a provider, workers' compensation, and other essential pensions.

Health and Safety Protections

The health and safety of gig workers are inevitable, given that their work may involve various activities in unexpected occurrences. Here's how policies and initiatives are being shaped to protect gig workers:

Safety Standards and Protections

Regulatory Frameworks: By putting in place regulations that provide gigs with health and safety concerns like traditional employees. It involves compliance with occupational safety standards and ensuring a safe working environment.

Training and Equipment: Gig platforms or clients must provide necessary training, information, and safety gear for gig workers, particularly in fields with potential health risks that require technical abilities.

Compensation for Work-Related Injuries: First, it makes sure that gig workers can receive payment or insurance requirements for injuries and illnesses caused by their work.

Mental Health Support

Access to Mental Health Resources: Providing mental health resources, such as counseling services, stress management programs, or digital support communities, acknowledges the specificity of the mental challenges that come with gig work.

Awareness and Education: However, to create awareness among gig workers and provide educational materials to help them identify symptoms of stress burnout or mental health disorders to seek suitable assistance.

Fair and Transparent Contracting

Contracting must be fair to safeguard gig workers' rights and ensure clarity and fairness in gig working arrangements. Here's how policies are fostering fair contracting practices:

Clear Contract Terms

Standardized Contracts: Supporting or implementing standardized contract templates specifying the terms of work, performance expectations, payment schedules, and gig worker rights for transparency in understanding.

Informed Consent: Ensure that you are fully informed and consent to the contract before any gig work begins, thus avoiding miscommunication or taking advantage.

Dispute Resolution and Advocacy

Accessible Dispute Resolution Mechanisms: Building employee-friendly mechanisms for addressing matters such as reporting grievances, issues, or mistakes and seeking redress in cases involving gig workers against the platforms or clients.

Advocacy and Legal Support: By offering advocacy services or creating avenues through which they can seek the necessary legal support in case of contract disputes, grievances, etc.

Tax and Financial Guidance

Managing taxes and financials is difficult for gig workers because they have to deal with many gigs and changing incomes. Here's how policies and initiatives can offer essential guidance and support:

Tax Guidance for Gig Workers

Clear, Accessible Information: offering information in tabular form about tax obligations, reporting income from gig work, the correct deductions, and deadlines.

Tailored Resources and Tools: Providing customized resources like online calculators, webinars, and guides to help gig workers manage their taxes.

Advisory Services: Gig workers should be able to access cheap or free tax advisory forums to receive specialized recommendations and guidance on filing taxes.

Financial Literacy and Support

Financial Education Programs: We are introducing financial literacy programs that address budgeting, saving, investing, and income stream irregularities.

Access to Financial Services: Enabling access to financial services and products that meet the needs of gig workers, like flexible savings schemes or insurance plans with adjustable premiums.

Retirement Planning: Providing information on and resources to gig workers for retirement planning, including how they can set up and contribute towards their future through contributions while working with a fluctuating income.

Promoting Skill Development and Career Growth

In an ever-changing job environment, gig workers need continuous skill development and employment expansion prospects to sustain market competitiveness and achieve their professional ambitions. Here's how support can be structured:

Access to Training and Upskilling

Subsidized Training Programs: These low-priced training programs allow gig workers to acquire new skills, remain abreast of industry trends, and improve their employability.

Flexible Learning Options: Providing flexible, personalized learning schemes for gig workers that enable them to achieve a work-life balance, including professional advancements.

Career Development Resources

Career Counseling Services: Providing career coaching services aimed at guiding gig workers on their paths, finding options for further development, and helping them make the right decisions regarding their professional path.

Networking Opportunities: Organize networking sessions or platforms through which gig workers can interact with peers, industry experts, and potential clients, thereby increasing their visibility and chances of collaboration.

Support for Entrepreneurial Ventures: Creating opportunities for gig workers who desire to venture into entrepreneurship through entrepreneurial resources such as mentorship, funding, and business development programs.

Safety Net Initiatives

These are indispensable if stability and security are to be provided to workers in the gig economy era, besides the broader job market that has witnessed a dramatic change over time away from traditional form. These programs are designed to safeguard workers from uncertainties and risks related to financial difficulties due to unemployment, sickness, or unexpected calamities. Here's how safety net initiatives can be structured and implemented:

Unemployment Insurance and Benefits

Include gig workers and individuals in non-conventional employment in unemployment insurance schemes. This requires rediscovering eligibility criteria to consider how gig work is done. Provide emergency funds or short-term employment support programs for employees who are made redundant due to recessions, disruptive technology shifts, and other emergencies.

Health Insurance and Medical Benefits

Make quality health insurance available to gig workers at affordable prices for them. Look at partnership models, including the government, private insurance companies, and gig platforms, to customize health plans specific to freelance work.

Retirement Savings and Pension Plans

Support the integration of gig workers into national pension programs or provide ways for gig platforms to contribute to retirement savings funds with match contributions, at least subsidized through government grants. Offer incentives or subsidies to motivate and support gig workers in preparing for retirement, acknowledging the problems of fluctuating income streams.

Income Stabilization Tools

Consider building income stability tools like wage insurance or averaging programs to help American gig workers handle periods of low earnings. Provide financial planning and budgeting tools to help workers control their finances despite their dynamic income.

Worker Protection and Compensation

Increase workers' compensation by including gig workers, making it mandatory to cover them when they have injuries caused at work or occupational risks. Enact laws that would require gig platforms to pay safety and protection funds that can be used for workers in the event of prolonged illness, injury, or when they cannot perform.

Skills Development and Transition Support

Provide continuous learning and upskilling training to help individuals stay updated with changes in the job market. Offer career transition programs that include counseling, job search assistance, and retraining for those seeking to switch fields or professions.

Regulation of Automation and AI

Governments are also responsible for regulating artificial intelligence to ensure proper ethics in its development, deployment, and use (Valerio De Stefano et al., 2022). Given the fast-moving nature of AI technology and its many challenges and opportunities, there is a need to find elegant but proactive regulatory frameworks. Here's how governments are addressing the task of regulating AI:

Developing Ethical Guidelines for AI

The development and use of AI have greatly impacted many facets of society and the economy. Establishing ethical guidelines is crucial to ensuring that these technologies are harnessed responsibly.

Crafting Ethical Principles for AI

Develop a universal code of ethics to govern the development and utilization of AI. This code typically encompasses principles such as fairness, non-discrimination, transparency, privacy, and protection of individual rights. Ensure that a diverse group of stakeholders, including ethicists, technologists, policymakers, and community representatives, actively participate in crafting these guidelines to reflect a broad spectrum of perspectives and concerns.

Operationalizing Ethical AI

Translate ethical principles into practical standards applicable throughout various stages of AI development, from design to deployment and monitoring. Establish universal standards and best practices for both AI developers and end-users. This framework should guide the ethical deployment of artificial intelligence, ensuring responsible and accountable use across all applications and industries.

Regulatory and Legal Frameworks

Regulatory mechanisms are essential to enforce compliance with ethical standards in AI development and use. These mechanisms may include legislation, regulatory organizations, or industry standards that mandate adherence to ethical principles. It's crucial to ensure that legal systems can address AI-related challenges by updating laws and regulations to keep pace with technological advancements.

Ensuring Transparency and Explainability

Transparency and accountability are the bases for building trust in AI systems. They ensure that AI decisions can be understood and scrutinized.

Transparency in AI Systems

Transparency is crucial for AI systems. Users should have access to information about how they function, the data they use, and the reasoning behind decisions made. Encouraging the adoption of open-source AI models or disclosing model architectures can improve transparency and facilitate peer review.

Explainability of AI Decisions

Create artificially intelligent systems that are truthful in their decisions and understandable to end-users. This is especially important in industries that greatly influence people's lives, such as healthcare, criminal justice, and finance. Promote methods for interpreting models or easy-to-use explanation tools that help make AI systems more understandable.

Protecting Data Privacy and Security

With data being a core asset for AI development in today's age, protecting its privacy and security becomes essential. Governments and regulatory bodies are significant in setting up frameworks and regulations that prevent data abuse or breaches. Here's how this can be approached:

Enforcement of Data Protection Laws

Strong data protection laws should be established and enforced to establish a universal framework for the collection, processing, storage, and sharing of information. Such laws should also guarantee the care and respect for privacy of personal and sensitive data. Provide specific guidelines on obtaining informed consent to collect their data and let them know how they will use the information obtained.

Securing Data Infrastructure

Strict security measures are required to protect the data infrastructure from possible breaches, leaks, or unauthorized uses. These measures encompass encryption, routine security audits, and cybersecurity best practices. Ensure that data storage and transmissions are safe according to the most stringent recommendations for protecting personal information.

Empowering Individuals with Data Control

Give individuals the right to manage their personal data, such as rights of access, correction, and deletion. Create structures enabling people to know what is done with their data and by whom so they can decide whether to share their information.

Addressing Bias and Discrimination

Bias and discrimination in AI systems can result in an unfair effect on people. It is necessary to address these problems proactively so that AI technologies become just and fair. Here's how bias and discrimination can be mitigated in AI:

Rigorous Testing for Bias

Mandate that AI models are thoroughly tested for bias and discrimination before release. This also involves experimentation with various datasets to ensure the system's decisions are consistent and not biased towards some groups. Incorporate continuous monitoring mechanisms that can detect and respond to biases that may arise as AI systems engage real-world data and situations.

Corrective Measures and Algorithmic Adjustments

Corrective actions are essential to address biases or discriminatory tendencies in AI systems. These may involve adjusting algorithms, training models with diverse data sets, or revising decision-making frameworks. Additionally, promoting transparency in algorithmic decision-making processes can facilitate identifying and rectifying biases.

Fostering Innovation While Ensuring Safety

In the rapidly advancing field of artificial intelligence, striking a balance between innovation, safety, and ethics is paramount. Governments and regulatory bodies play a crucial role in fostering "innovation ecosystems" that encourage innovation while safeguarding the public interest. Here's how this delicate balance can be achieved:

Promoting Responsible Innovation

Encourage the cultivation of responsible AI development practices among developers and companies, emphasizing consideration of moral, social, and safety implications.

Offer incentives for creating AI solutions that address societal challenges, improve quality of life, and positively impact human well-being, reinforcing the connection between innovation and ethics.

Regulatory Sandboxes and Innovation Hubs

Create regulatory sandboxes or innovation hubs where AI innovators can safely develop and test emerging technologies under close supervision. This enables practical assessment of the technology's effects, benefits, and risks. Provide guidance, tools, and support within these sandboxes, encouraging innovators to explore new ideas while adhering to regulatory and ethical standards.

Promoting Collaboration and Global Standards

International collaboration and consensus on standards and regulations for AI are imperative. With AI technologies transcending national borders, countries must work together to establish a unified and comprehensive framework for AI governance. Here's how this can be fostered:

International Dialogues and Collaborations

Engage in global dialogues and collaborations to exchange insights, best practices, and challenges in AI governance. By sharing diverse perspectives and cultural insights, the global community can better understand AI's implications. Advocate for developing AI regulations and standards that prioritize the well-being of all communities worldwide.

Participation in Global Forums and Treaties

Participate actively in global forums, working groups, and treaties focused on AI to ensure the representation of national views and interests in the worldwide discourse on AI governance.

Contribute to the development of international policies, principles, and treaties that establish ethical guidelines for AI implementation. Shared global standards can address data privacy, security, and AI equity challenges.

Policies Encouraging Lifelong Learning

In the current dynamic job market, where skill needs constantly change, government policies that support continuous learning are required. These policies are critical to promoting a robust, flexible workforce to address future challenges while capturing opportunities. Here's how governments can and are supporting continuous learning:

Lifelong Learning Initiatives

Implement national strategies for lifelong learning to encourage continuous skill development throughout individuals' careers. These strategies include raising public awareness, offering incentives for ongoing education, and fostering a culture that values lifelong learning. Additionally, support adult education centers, online learning platforms, and community colleges to provide accessible options for working learners.

Subsidies and Financial Support for Training

Provide subsidies, tax incentives, or vouchers to individuals and employers to mitigate the cost of training programs and professional development courses. This removes the economic restriction on accessing education and motivates employees and employers to invest in talent development. Create education savings accounts or offer discounted loans to those interested in continuing their studies.

Partnerships With Educational Institutions and Industry

Promote collaboration between the government, educational centers, and industry so that learning programs are responsive to current and future market needs. This entails continuous conversation and cooperation to revise curricula and create new programs focusing on filling workforce skill gaps. To support apprenticeship and internship programs that offer practical training alongside formal education.

Digital Literacy and Access

Support projects that increase digital literacy among all citizens as users so that they have the basic skills to work in a more and more virtual environment. Invest in digital infrastructure and ensure that online learning platforms are available, affordable, or even accessible for students to access.

Recognition and Accreditation of Skills

Create skill and qualification recognition and accreditation systems for non-traditional learning paths, including online courses, workshops, or self-study. This will ensure that all forms of learning are also appreciated and recognized on the job market. Promote digital badges or portable credentials that people can obtain and display as a token of their efforts throughout their careers.

Support for Transitioning Workers

Comprehensive educational incentive programs are crucial to support the retraining and reskilling of workers transitioning between industries or those impacted by automation. These programs encourage individuals, companies, and educational institutions to invest in skill development continuously throughout their lives. Here's how incentives can be structured to promote educational initiatives:

Tax Incentives for Individuals and Employers

Tax incentives are a powerful method for encouraging investment in education, reducing the financial burden of continuous learning, and promoting a culture of lifelong education. Here's a closer look at how these incentives can be structured:

Tax credits, savings accounts, grants, subsidies, and loan assistance programs are all financial tools available to individuals and employers to facilitate education and training. These incentives are crucial in advancing individual skills and fostering the development of a highly skilled workforce.

For Individuals

Individual Tax Credits or Deductions: People can receive much from tax credits or deductions for education and training-associated costs. This entails a wide range of learning activities, such as attendance in part-time studies, evening classes, online learning, and certifications, whereby costs incurred as tuition fees and purchase of learning materials are included.

Lifelong Learning Accounts: Establishing a tax-free savings account allocated to future educational and training costs mandates people to put a part of their income into personal development. The money you put in such accounts is either tax-deductible or your interest is paid tax-free, making such savings vehicles tempting for continuing education and skill enrichment.

For Employers

Training Tax Credits for Employers: Training tax credits incentivize employers to invest in their workforce's continued development. This program helps employers provide in-house training programs, pay for externally sponsored learning, or support apprenticeships, all of which lead to improved skills or productivity of the employees.

Tax Benefits for Collaborative Training Initiatives: To further foster industry-specific training, companies that co-operate with education setups or organizations to develop customized training modules to match the skills of their labor force to those dictated by the needs of a particular industry are offered even more significant sums of tax break.

Grants and Subsidies for Education and Training

Grants and subsidies provide direct financial assistance, making education and training more affordable for individuals or groups who might otherwise struggle with the cost.

For Individuals

Grants for education and scholarship programs partially or fully cover the cost of education and training. They can be merit-based or need-based and often target particular populations—for instance, returning students, low-income families, or those entering in-demand professions. Subsidies for vocational and technical training programs ensure that individuals obtain skills that suit current, trending, and future job markets.

For Educational Institutions and Training Providers

Funding is offered in program development, facilitating institutions and training providers to create and deliver programs compliant with industry requirements and address skill deficiencies.

Student Loan Assistance and Forgiveness Programs

Unburdening graduates, particularly those in employment-critical sectors, is an essential course of action. Loan support and forgiveness programs, designed to ease people from such a burden, manage this load.

Loan Assistance Programs

Student loans become more affordable with interest rate reductions, but this does not necessarily target the whole population but specific categories such as graduates in public services or those in high demand by the industry. The fact that the rejected persons may pursue further education, start a business, or experience a financial crisis does not imply that the loan repayment is a factor that hinders their career advancement or economic recovery, which explains why deferred payment options are offered to the graduates to enable them to continue.

Loan Forgiveness Programs

Public Service Loan Forgiveness programs aim to alleviate or eliminate debt, offering total forgiveness for graduates who work in public service positions after a specified period. These programs attract qualified individuals to vital roles in society. Similarly, wedlock schemes provide debt relief for graduates serving in underserved areas and essential industries.

In summary, various approaches, such as tax incentives, savings accounts, grants, subsidies, and loan programs, can foster a culture of lifelong learning and skill improvement. These financial mechanisms empower individuals to pursue education and ensure employers have skilled workers, aligning talent development with industry needs and societal progress.

Portable Credentialing and Certification Systems

As the job market evolves rapidly, accumulating and carrying credentials becomes increasingly essential for lifelong learning and career mobility. Here's how governments can support the development of portable credentialing and certification systems:

Development of Portable Systems

Inter-Institutional Credit Transfer: Encourage programs that enable credit portability so learners can easily transition from program to program or institution without giving up the ground gained.

Digital Credential Platforms: Invest in creating digital platforms that safely keep and share credentials, allowing learners to maintain an updated, portable record of their learning accomplishments.

Incentives for Certification and Credentialing

Recognition of Industry Certifications: Promote the integration of industry-recognized certifications or credentials in the formal education track to warrant practical, job-related skills and academic credits.

Incentives for Continuous Learning: Provide incentives, including tax deductions or subsidies for individuals who acquire industry-recognized certifications and those undertaking continuous professional development, to show that lifelong learning is vital in career progression.

Portable Credentialing and Certification Systems

The ability to gather and carry credentials from different sources over time is precious in a changing job market. Let's take a closer look at how we can support and encourage portable credentialing and certification systems:

Support for System Development

Interoperable Credentialing Platforms: Invest in the deployment of secure platforms that are interoperable. This will enable the storage, management, and sharing of digital credentials and help ensure the portability of credentials between organizations and sectors.

Standardization of Credits and Certifications: Pursue the traditionalization of credits and certificates in educational institutions and training programs to ensure that they are easy for learners to transfer from one place to another while still maintaining their value or relevance.

Incentives for Credential Acquisition

Subsidies or Tax Benefits: Incentivize individuals pursuing industry-accepted certifications or credentials. This can assist in covering the cost of exams, learning materials, and even courses, making it less expensive for individuals to invest in their career development.

Portable Credentialing and Certification Systems

Recognition in Career Advancement: Include qualifications recognized by industry certificates and credentials in career progression within an organization, motivating workers to have those qualities.

Workplace Learning and Development Programs

Fostering lifelong learning within the workplace is critical in helping employees' abilities remain relevant and businesses to be competitive. Here's how workplace learning and development programs can be encouraged and structured:

Encouraging Employer Investment

Financial Incentives for Employers: Offer tax incentives, subsidies, or grants to businesses interested in investing more time and resources into employee training programs. This could offset the costs and make more employers offer learning opportunities.

Recognition Programs: Create recognition programs or award companies that achieve positive employee training and development results, share best practices, and support a continuous learning culture.

Fostering Industry-Education Partnerships

Collaborative Curriculum Development: Support collaboration between private sectors and academic institutions to jointly develop curricula that meet current and future needs. This guarantees the provision of relevant, practical skills that will be used at the workplace.

Practical Learning Opportunities: Promote apprenticeships, internships, and mentoring programs that provide practical learning opportunities. Organizations that provide these opportunities can be provided with financial incentives or support to ensure that students and job seekers acquire industry exposure.

Conclusion

In wrapping up this chapter, it's evident that governments play a crucial role in shaping an inclusive, innovative, and resilient future of work. The policies discussed go beyond mere reactions to change; they represent proactive steps toward fostering an agile workforce and promoting workplace equality. Cooperation between policymakers and businesses is essential, as it allows for a shared vision and flexible adaptation to build for the future of work.

Chapter 10: Entrepreneurship in the New Work Landscape

Entrepreneurship is crucial in navigating the challenges of today's labor sector, offering a beacon of hope amid uncertainty. This chapter explores how successful entrepreneurs thrive in the ever-changing business landscape, emphasizing the importance of agility, innovation, and perseverance in realizing their visions. These entrepreneurs redefine traditional norms, setting new standards and blazing unique paths to success. The chapter celebrates their victories and delves into their mindset, strategies, and resilience in overcoming challenges and embracing change. It highlights the need for education, access to capital, and supportive regulatory environments to foster entrepreneurial growth (Edghiem et al., 2023).

Entrepreneurial Opportunities in Emerging Industries

Emerging sectors offer fertile ground for entrepreneurial ventures due to innovations, technological advancements, and evolving consumer preferences. These industries emerge from societal needs, technological capabilities, and market gaps, giving entrepreneurs a blank canvas to build successful businesses. Here's how entrepreneurs can seize opportunities in emerging sectors:

Technology and Innovation-Driven Sectors

Artificial Intelligence and Machine Learning: Start-ups can create AI-driven solutions in healthcare, finance, education, etc., providing products based on predictive analytics and personalized customer experiences.

Clean Tech and Renewable Energy: As we increasingly pursue sustainable development, entrepreneurs find more areas to innovate, such as renewable energy and waste management, for a greener economy.

Health and Wellness

Telemedicine and Digital Health: The healthcare industry is an ideal ground for disruption, where potential opportunities can be found within telehealth platforms, wearable health tech, and personalized medicine, addressing the growing need to make health care more conveniently available.

Mental Health and Well-Being: With increasing awareness and the demand for mental health services, some prospects open up opportunities to various platforms providing counseling products and mindfulness programs.

Consumer-Oriented Sectors

E-Commerce and Direct-to-Consumer Models: The change in consumer shopping behaviors paves the way for niche e-commerce sites and direct-to-consumer brands that sell customizable products with unique experiences, subscription boxes, etc.

Food Technology: Innovations in food technology, such as plant-based alternatives, sustainable packaging, and the introduction of on-demand delivery systems, serve to meet changing consumer attitudes regarding sustainability and convenience.

Education and EdTech

Online Learning Platforms and Tools: The digitization of education creates opportunities for developing online platforms, interactive learning tools, and educational content to meet the varied needs and preferences for different types of learning.

Lifelong Learning and Upskilling: The demand for continuous learning creates an opportunity for potential entrepreneurs who need to explore the market by providing professional development courses, skill certification programs, and career coaching services.

Financial Services and FinTech

Digital Banking and Payment Solutions: The FinTech sector has opportunities in digital banking services, payment processing solutions, and financial management tools that provide convenience, security, and customized financial facilities.

Blockchain and Cryptocurrency: Blockchain technology and digital currencies offer opportunities for entrepreneurs to create decentralized finance (DeFi), smart contracts, and secure transaction platforms. One essential skill for entrepreneurs is identifying and addressing market gaps where demand exceeds supply. Successfully managing these gaps can lead to significant entrepreneurial success. Here's how entrepreneurs can recognize and take advantage of market gaps:

Market Research and Analysis

Understanding Consumer Needs: Conduct surveys, focus groups, and market analysis to determine consumer needs, wants, and pain points. A customer review of the current products and services can also identify unmet needs.

Competitive Analysis: Compare the competitive environment and point out places where competitors do not meet all customer needs or when there is no competition.

Trend Monitoring and Forecasting

Stay Informed of Industry Trends: Stay updated on the latest trends, innovations in technology, and changes being implemented by regulatory bodies within your industry. This may uncover new prospects and possible market holes.

Predict Future Needs: Then, use trend analysis and forecasting tools to determine the market direction where new demands or preferences might emerge.

Innovative Thinking and Creativity

Think outside the Box: Promote creativity and innovation in your team. Sometimes, another person's perspective or novel approach can highlight the gaps others missed.

Prototype and Iterate: Create prototypes and test them with your potential users to get feedback. This iterative process can continue to refine the product or service to match better what is needed in the market.

Building a Strong Value Proposition

Highlight Unique Benefits: Ensure that your product or service provides unique benefits not currently available in the market. Communicate this value proposition clearly to your target audience.

Focus On Quality and Customer Experience: In industries where products and customer service are not up to par, firms can gain market share by being high in both areas as well.

Leveraging Technology and Data

Use Data Analytics: Use data analytics programs to analyze market information, consumer patterns, and trends in the industry. These insights can be used to uncover market gaps and consumer needs that are not addressed sufficiently.

Adopt Emerging Technologies: Use new technologies to create unique solutions that address market gaps. For example, using AI to provide personalized product recommendations or VR for immersive shopping can differentiate your offering.

Strategic Partnerships and Collaboration

Form Strategic Alliances: Partner with other companies, research institutions, or start-ups to pool expertise, assets, and market power. By forming partnerships, it may be possible to delve into unexplored markets or create solutions that will better address the gaps in various markets.

Engage with the Community: Engaging with your community can give you an invaluable window into local needs and preferences, which will help you determine what market gaps need to be addressed.

Navigating Risk and Uncertainty

Being an entrepreneur means dealing with risks. Successful entrepreneurs usually handle, minimize, and even embrace risks. To develop a robust risk-management strategy, entrepreneurs must be aware of possible mistakes, make intelligent decisions, and prepare backup plans. Here's how entrepreneurs can manage risks effectively:

Conduct Thorough Market Research

Understand Your Market: Research market demand, customer preferences, competition, and industry trends before starting a new venture. This data enables you to make more informed choices and minimizes the chances of plunging into a non-profitable market.

Validate Your Idea: Analyze your business idea using tools such as surveys, focus groups, or MVPs to get confirmation from the target audience. Feedback allows you to improve your product or service and lessen the possibility of rejection by the market.

Financial Planning and Management

Create a Solid Business Plan: Write a detailed business plan, including financial projections, marketing strategies, and operational plans. A good strategy can be a guide and help predict shocks.

Manage Cash Flow: Good cash flow management should ensure you have enough capital to fund running costs and contingencies. Keep a budget and regularly check your financial statements if you wish to have complete control over your finances.

Risk Assessment and Mitigation

Identify Potential Risks: You need to systematically identify potential threats facing the business in terms of market risks, financial risks, regulatory risks, and operational risks.

Develop Risk Mitigation Strategies: Formulate mitigation strategies for every risk you have identified. This may involve product range diversification, obtaining insurance coverage, or enacting strict compliance policies.

Build a Resilient Team

Hire the Right People: Assemble a team with diverse skill sets and backgrounds. A mixed team can offer new insights into challenges and devise creative solutions for them.

Foster a Culture of Open Communication: Promote open communication in your team. Comfortable team members can detect problems early and propose various risk mitigation strategies.

Leverage Technology and Data

Use Data Analytics: Use data analytics to understand customer behavior, market trends, and operations efficiency. Data-based decisions may help avoid expensive mistakes.

Invest in Technology: Apply technology to streamline business processes, enhance customer engagement, and create efficiencies. Leading in tech adoption is a way to improve your competitive position and reduce the threat of lagging.

Develop Contingency Plans

Have Backup Plans: Make contingencies in case of unexpected occurrences. This could be through backup suppliers, contingency funds, or alternate operational strategies.

Regularly Review and Update Your Plans: The business environment is dynamic. Keep your risk management strategies and contingency plans current.

Network and Seek Advice

Build a Support Network: Create a circle of mentors, advisers, and fellow entrepreneurs. Their knowledge and observations are priceless in guiding you through risks and making prudent decisions.

Learn From Failures: To handle failures, see them as chances to learn. Determine what went wrong, adjust your plans, and move forward with new insights.

To manage risks in entrepreneurship, stay active and keep learning. Be ready to respond quickly and effectively. Understanding the landscape, careful planning, and fostering resilience help entrepreneurs navigate challenges and steer their businesses toward stability.

Resilience is crucial for entrepreneurs, helping them endure business challenges positively. It's about enduring tough times and adapting, evolving, and improving. Here's how entrepreneurs can develop resilience skills and mindset:

Adaptability and Flexibility

Embrace Change: Nurture a perception of change as an opportunity rather than a threat. Be prepared to redirect your strategies, look for new markets, or modify your products due to shifting circumstances.

Learn From Experience: Past experiences can offer learning opportunities, both successes and failures. Evaluate which elements were successful, what failed, and how those things could be applied during future struggles.

Emotional Intelligence

Self-Awareness: Cultivate a deep understanding of your strengths, weaknesses, feelings, and triggers. Self-awareness makes it possible to manage one's emotions responsibly and make reasonable decisions.

Empathy: Practice empathy toward your team, customers, and stakeholders. Accepting other people's points of view can build fundamental relationships during difficult times.

Perseverance and Tenacity

Set Long-Term Goals: Stay focused on your long-term goals, in spite of momentary challenges. This will help you keep focus and direction in times of turbulence.

Show Grit: Demonstrate tenacity and determination. Be aware that failures are inevitable, but determination is essential to success.

Strategic Problem-Solving

Analytical Thinking: Learn how to analyze intricate situations, pick out crucial issues, and determine the true potential of alternative scenarios. This skill is necessary in decision-making under pressure.

Creative Solutions: Support creative problem-solving. Alternative methods can sometimes result in successful solutions during difficult periods.

Effective Communication

Clear and Transparent Communication: Stay in contact with your team, partners, and stakeholders. Open communication builds trust and ensures that everyone is on the same page in terms of alignment, but most importantly, during emergencies.

Active Listening: To make this statement, actively listen to others' concerns, ideas, and feedback. This may offer meaningful information and assist in making broader, more inclusive decisions.

Mindfulness and Stress Management

Mindfulness Practices: Practice mindfulness activities like meditation, yoga, or deep breath work. These activities help preserve clear thinking and low-stress levels.

Work-Life Balance: Aim for a balanced working life. Taking time to rest and recharge is not a privilege; it's essential for sustaining resilience and success in the long run.

Continuous Learning and Growth Mindset

Lifelong Learning: Commit to lifelong learning and skill development. Stay up-to-date on what is happening in your trade, emerging technology, and management styles so you don't limit yourself or the business.

Growth Mindset: Develop a mindset that views challenges as opportunities for development and knowledge. This attitude fosters resilience, as it defines failures in terms of the learning and development process.

By developing these skills and promoting a resilient mindset, entrepreneurs can confidently face the challenges of today's business world, where difficulties become opportunities for creativity, innovation, and sustained prosperity.

The Role of Technology in Entrepreneurship

Technology is vital in supporting entrepreneurship by acting as an innovation, growth, and niche engine. Technology provides entrepreneurs various instruments and platforms in the digital era to convert ideas into viable businesses. Here's an examination of how technology is shaping and empowering entrepreneurship:

Ease of Starting a Business

Digital Tools and Platforms: Digital tools and platforms developed with user-friendliness in mind have considerably helped lower the barriers to entry into business. This is possible because of technology that has transformed how people live and work.

Access to Resources and Information: The Internet has great resources, mostly including online tutorials and courses, discussion boards, and communities where entrepreneurs can learn and interact with others.

Market Reach and Customer Engagement

E-Commerce Platforms: Technology allows businesses to reach a worldwide market while eliminating the need for brick-and-mortar stores. E-commerce platforms enable entrepreneurs to display and sell their products in a vast market.

Social Media and Digital Marketing: Social media sites and digital marketing tools enable entrepreneurs to communicate with their audience, create brand recognition, and cost-effectively promote products.

Product Development and Innovation

Rapid Prototyping and 3D Printing: Technologies such as 3D printing allow entrepreneurs to rapidly prototype ideas and iterate designs, consequently shortening product development accordingly.

AI and Machine Learning: These technologies can give entrepreneurs knowledge of customer behavior and process optimization and even push innovation in products and services.

Operational Efficiency and Automation

Business Process Automation: Automated tools can help entrepreneurs save precious time and minimize costs. This ranges from automated customer support via chatbots to accounting software.

Cloud Computing: Cloud services allow entrepreneurs to have scalable, customizable, and affordable data storage, application hosting, and collaboration solutions, eliminating the high costs of setting up a robust IT infrastructure.

Funding and Financial Management

Crowdfunding Platforms: Websites such as Kickstarter and Indiegogo offer entrepreneurs an alternative to traditional funding routes, such as bank loans or venture capital firms.

Financial Tech (FinTech): FinTech solutions provide entrepreneurs with advanced tools to manage their finances, including mobile banking and payments, financial analytics, and forecasting.

Networking and Collaboration

Online Networking Platforms: Entrepreneurs can easily form connections with peers, mentors, investors, and potential partners through websites such as LinkedIn.

Collaboration Tools: Applications such as Slack, Trello, and Asana allow entrepreneurs to manage projects conveniently while simultaneously keeping their teams harmonious no matter where they might be.

Digital tools and e-commerce platforms have brought an incredible revolution in how entrepreneurs run their businesses, making it possible to achieve unparalleled growth efficiency and customer reach. Here's a closer look at how these tools are shaping entrepreneurship:

Digital Tools for Business Operations

Project Management and Collaboration Tools

Tools such as Asana, Trello, and Monday.com make project management more efficient by supporting team collaboration processes. They allow entrepreneurs to schedule tasks, set timelines, monitor progress, and ensure that all team members are on board in terms of knowledge.

Customer Relationship Management (CRM) Systems

CRM systems such as Salesforce, HubSpot, and Zoho CRM allow entrepreneurs to control their interactions with existing or potential customers. These systems assist in managing client data, monitoring sales engagements, and automating marketing programs.

Financial Management and Accounting Software

Software such as QuickBooks, Xero, and Freshbooks help streamline entrepreneurs' financial management. They help with invoicing, expense tracking, payroll processing, and delivering financial insights through dashboards and reports.

Communication and Conferencing Tools

Essential internal and external communication tools like Slack, Zoom, and Microsoft Teams have been created. They enable instant messaging, video conferencing, and file sharing, making communication easier no matter where both parties are located.

E-commerce Platforms and Tools

Online Marketplaces and E-Commerce Platforms

Platforms such as Amazon, eBay, Shopify, and WooCommerce allow users to quickly create online stores that attract international customers. These platforms offer various services, such as web hosting, shopping cart integration, transaction processing, and customer support.

Digital Marketing and SEO Tools

Tools such as Google Ads, Facebook Ads Manager, and SEMrush allow entrepreneurs to market their products properly. They help in building, managing, and optimizing ad campaigns, keyword research, and enhancing search engine rankings.

Analytics and Data Insights Tools

Google Analytics, Mixpanel, or Hotjar are analytics tools that deliver information on customer behavior, website performance, and conversion rates. Entrepreneurs can use this information to make informed decisions and analyze their marketing strategy, enhancing user experience.

Social Media Management Tools

Entrepreneurs use tools like Hootsuite, Buffer, and Sprout Social to manage their social media presence. These tools enable the scheduling of posts, monitoring of social media engagements, and measuring performance on various platforms.

Conclusion

In this chapter, we've learned that entrepreneurship today is about blending creativity, strategy, passion, and adaptability. It involves embracing technology, constantly learning, and staying resilient in tough times. As we end this chapter, we carry valuable lessons and inspiration to embrace change and seize opportunities. The future belongs to those who dare to dream, make decisions, and take the first step into uncharted territory, armed with knowledge, innovation, and an entrepreneurial mindset.

Chapter 11: The Road Ahead: Strategies for Individuals and Organizations

The future requires a new approach, blending ongoing learning, adaptability, and resilience. Individuals must embrace continuous learning, flexibility, and the ability to bounce back from challenges. Organizations should foster cultures of creativity, create adaptable systems, and develop strategies that extend beyond current horizons.

This chapter serves as more than just a signpost; it's a roadmap for the future of work. It covers leadership, collaboration, and understanding the forces shaping our world—from technological advancements to changing market trends and evolving values. It's about harnessing potential disruptions as opportunities for growth and aligning individual aspirations with organizational strategies.

It's a narrative of what could be, what might happen, and what's at stake. It invites you to delve into your passions, where every step brings experience and influence, pushing you to higher levels. Let's embark on a journey to explore ways to transform individuals and businesses into remarkable forces in this ever-changing landscape—not just with security but with a spark of creativity that redefines success.

Personal Development Plans for Career Agility

Personal development planning is a strategic procedure that helps people who wish to develop personally and professionally. It includes self-evaluation, target setting, and planning the route to develop skills, experiences, and capabilities. Here's a guide to help individuals craft effective personal development plans:

Self-Assessment and Reflection

Identify Strengths and Weaknesses: Inventory your current skill sets, competencies, and limitations. SWOT analysis (Strengths, Weaknesses, Opportunities, Threats) can be helpful in this phase.

Understand Your Passions and Values: Think about your passions and the values that you hold dear. This perception will help you to establish realistic goals that are also rewarding.

Setting Clear and Realistic Goals

Define Short-Term and Long-Term Goals: Establish SMART objectives. Separate short and long-term goals from objectives.

Align Goals with Career Aspirations: Make sure that your goals reflect where you see yourself in the future. Think of how each goal will lead to your professional development.

Planning for Skill Development

Identify Required Skills and Knowledge: By your objectives, specify what skills should be acquired or improved.

Choose Learning and Development Activities: Choose suitable learning and development activities for each skill or knowledge area. This might involve formal education, online training, workshops or webinars, and self-study.

Seeking Mentorship and Feedback

Find a Mentor or Coach: Find mentors or coaches who can provide guidance, feedback, and encouragement as they support your quest to achieve concrete goals. They can also provide useful guidance and suggestions based on their professional backgrounds.

Embrace Constructive Feedback: Get feedback from your peers, bosses, or mentors. Positive feedback can also offer another point of view and help you complete your development plan.

Creating an Action Plan

Outline Action Steps: Divide every goal into actionable tasks. Set deadlines and prioritize tasks to keep the flow going.

Allocate Resources: Decide what you need to finish each action step, whether that means time, money, or other people's support. Schedule how you will use these resources wisely.

Monitoring Progress and Adjusting the Plan

Regularly Review Your Plan: Schedule time to assess your progress regularly. Remember what you have achieved and whether it is necessary to readjust your goals.

Stay Flexible and Adaptive: Be ready to change your plan when the situation changes or you learn more about it.

Self-evaluation is the pillar of personal and professional development, which leads to continuous learning and constitutes the foundation for successful careers based on lived-out lives. They allow people to stay competitive, flexible, and grounded in their fundamental values and goals. Here's an emphasis on the importance of self-assessment and continuous learning:

The Power of Self-Assessment

1. *Understanding Your Starting Point*

Understand that self-assessment is the first stage of personal growth. It gives you a realistic picture of your current location, allowing you to plan your future destination. Personality tests, skill assessments, and peer feedback can provide critical information.

2. *Identifying Strengths and Areas for Improvement*

Leverage your strengths using the self-assessment process. It is as important as identifying areas for improvement that you want to keep in mind while trying to be wholesome.

3. Aligning with Personal Values and Goals

Ensure that the career and life you choose align with your values and long-term objectives. Self-evaluation allows you to better coordinate your daily actions with larger life goals, leading to a happier and goal-driven way of living.

4. The Imperative of Continuous Learning

Embracing Change: In an always-evolving world, staying adaptable is crucial. Whether it's keeping up with new industry trends, advancements in technology, or shifts in the market, continuous learning helps you stay relevant.

Career Growth and Skill Building: Invest in your growth through lifelong learning. This can involve formal education, gaining professional qualifications, or taking advantage of informal learning opportunities like reading books or attending online workshops.

Fostering a Growth Mindset: Adopting a growth mindset means seeing challenges as opportunities for growth and learning. Recognize that skills and intelligence can be developed through effort and persistence.

Broadening Perspectives and Networks: Continuous learning often involves collaborating with mentors or peers in your industry. These interactions can expand your professional network and expose you to new ideas and perspectives.

Personal Satisfaction and Confidence: Learning new things keeps you engaged and boosts your confidence. It fosters innovation and may even lead to discovering new interests or passions.

Building Adaptive and Resilient Organizations

One of the most essential elements in ensuring an organization thrives within the current competitive business environment is creating a culture that can adapt. The characteristics of an adaptive culture include embracing change, promoting creativity, and developing a workforce ready to face the future. Here are some strategies for building adaptive cultures in organizations:

Foster a Growth Mindset

Encourage Learning: Develop a culture of continuous learning. Encourage employees to participate in professional development activities and ensure that they have access to the resources needed.

Embrace Failures as Learning Opportunities: Develop a culture where employees can try new things and learn from mistakes without fear of punishment. This will encourage innovation and experimentation.

Promote Flexibility and Agility

Flexible Work Policies: Provide work arrangements that are flexible enough to accommodate employees' lifestyles. This demonstrates that you trust your employees, and such an attitude may help boost workplace efficiency and job satisfaction.

Agile Decision-Making: Make decision-making processes efficient so that you can quickly respond to changing market demands. If appropriate, allow employees to decide matters at a lower level.

Open Communication Channels

Regular Feedback: Foster open communication channels for employees to share ideas, feedback, and concerns. Consistently interact with your team to get an insight into their struggles and requirements.

Transparency: Be open about company objectives, difficulties, and changes. If employees can understand the "why" behind decisions, they are more likely to support and adjust to change.

Cultivate Leadership at All Levels

Empowerment: Promote a culture where employees can lead projects or improvements. Such empowerment may also lead to engagement and a feeling of ownership.

Leadership Development: Invest in training programs that teach leaders to lead teams under volatile conditions.

Encourage Collaboration and Teamwork

Cross-Functional Teams: Promote cooperation of various departments and teams. This creates innovative solutions and improves the culture of unity in a business.

Diversity and Inclusion: Create an inclusive working environment that values various opinions. Diversity can result in better solutions and a more adaptive workforce.

Leverage Technology and Data

Digital Tools: Use digital tools that facilitate teamwork, project management, and communication. This can simplify operations and allow teams to collaborate more efficiently.

Data-Driven Insights: Make decisions and strategies based on data. Speedily interpreting and reacting to data can ensure that your organization is ahead of trends because it allows you to adapt appropriately.

Recognize and Reward Adaptability

Reward Innovation: Recognize and encourage employees who show flexibility, take initiative, or find creative solutions. This may strengthen a culture of continuous improvement.

Performance Metrics: Add flexibility and innovation to your performance measures. What is being measured gets managed, and incorporating these metrics can lead to an adaptive culture.

Building resilience within an organization is one of the most critical leadership functions, especially during change or instability. Resilient leaders do not just help their teams navigate challenges successfully but also make them stronger and more agile in the process. Here are critical leadership practices that can foster resilience:

Visionary and Strategic Thinking

Communicate a Clear Vision: Specify a powerful vision of the future. When employees know the bigger picture and where their work fits into it, they are likely to stay focused even during adversities.

Emphasize Strategic Priorities: Ensure that your team concentrates on what is relevant. Learning to prioritize can help people cope with being overwhelmed, and even when the unexpected happens, it enables them to stay on course.

Emotional Intelligence and Empathy

Practice Active Listening: Show your team you value their ideas, concerns, and feedback. Active listening is a great way to establish trust, discover underlying problems, and create an atmosphere of support.

Demonstrate Empathy: The emotional experiences of your team, especially during change or stressful situations, should be learned and considered. Through empathy, you can learn to handle difficult conversations and make decisions that consider the needs and perceptions of your team.

Effective Communication and Transparency

Provide Clear and Consistent Communication: Inform your team about changes, decisions, and plans. Transparency enhances trust and reduces uncertainties.

Encourage Open Dialogue: Create an atmosphere where employees feel comfortable sharing their concerns, ideas, and opinions. Good communication brings about innovative ideas and a feeling of purpose.

Empowerment and Delegation

Empower Your Team: Empower your team to act and make decisions within its influence. Empowerment enables faster problem resolution and an engaged workforce.

Delegate Effectively: Share roles and responsibilities using people's strengths to help them develop. Good delegation can make a team more robust and more resilient.

Encouraging Adaptability and Learning

Promote a Growth Mindset: Help your employees see challenges as learning points. Develop a culture that advocates for effort and continuous improvement.

Support Continuous Learning by Offering opportunities for professional growth. Teams that constantly upgrade their skills and knowledge can adjust quickly to change.

Building a Supportive Culture

Foster Team Cohesion: Foster teamwork and cooperation. A united team is more resilient and can support each other during adversity.

Recognize and Celebrate Achievements: Recognize individual and team successes, even small ones. Recognition can motivate employees and ingrain a culture of persistence.

Modelling Resilience

Lead by Example: Be resilient in your behavior. Leaders dealing with difficulties optimistically and innovatively inspire their team.

Maintain a Balanced Perspective: Beware of challenges and remain levelheaded. Cool-headed leaders often offer a counterbalance to agitated team members and can lead them through rough patches.

By using these leadership practices, leaders can create and cultivate an organization that is resilient to adversity, able to adapt in times of change, and able to grow stronger from challenges. Resilient leadership does not only imply survival through the storm but also establishing a direction that will make every team member sail with self-assurance into tomorrow.

Collaboration and Networking in the Digital Age

Collaboration and networking are imperative aspects of business today because they help employees grow professionally. At the same time, organizations continue accumulating into rising scales, not discounting innovation. In a world where globalization is exponentially increasing, collaborations play 'make or break' because one has to build formal and informal networks.

Importance of Collaboration

Pooling of Skills and Knowledge: Collaboration combines unique talents and knowledge bases into a group that assists the company. This diversity can bring about more innovative and comprehensive solutions to problems since different team members contribute unique perceptiveness.

Enhancing Innovation: Working together is an effective catalyst for innovation. Questions and solutions are tossed around, and new ways arise that may never have been achieved in solitude.

Increased Efficiency and Productivity: Collaboration tends to create better results in most cases because the workload among partners can be divided according to their skills. Working together creates an atmosphere of time-saving competitive drive that leads immediately to execution.

Learning and Development: Hiccups, working together offers scope for personal and professional development. Hiring team members to work with your knowledge develops a love of learning in other forms from acquired expertise.

Building a Supportive Work Culture: Collaboration generates unity and a sense of belonging among an organization's employees. It fosters open communication and trust, two critical elements in a conducive workplace ethos.

Importance of Networking

Access to Opportunities: Networking is associated with new opportunities that include employment offers, business initiatives, or treats, as well as entrepreneurial activities and labor bargaining. It's usually through networks that these opportunities are linked, and people learn about and find their way to them.

Knowledge and Information Exchange: Networking is a process of sharing information and ideas. Maintaining connections with a wide network of contacts will provide information on industry trends, successes, and innovation.

Resource and Support System: A good lineup can be an excellent support source, giving tips about what to do in case of imminent danger. Having a network of support can change lives, particularly during difficult periods.

Reputation and Influence Building: Networking is a mode that leads to building a reputation in the workplace and maintaining leadership while creating an influence in the domicile. This can help build credibility and acquire the ability to influence being in one's field.

Collaborative Partnerships: This process may develop partnerships based on different positions, and this cooperation will be mutually advantageous. The collaborations allow expansion of market frontiers, accrual and acquisition of more resources, and advancement in brand value.

In the digital age, leveraging online collaboration and networking platforms can bring significant benefits. Whether seeking professional connections or aiming to foster relationships with partners and customers, online platforms offer valuable opportunities for engagement and growth.

Choose the Right Platforms: Identify the online platforms that best suit your target audience and interests. For business owners, platforms like LinkedIn can help establish professional connections and gather industry insights. Twitter and other social media platforms are useful for staying updated on real-time industry trends. Platforms like Meetup can also help locate local events or join groups related to your interests.

Complete and Optimize Your Profiles: Make sure that you have all the necessary profiles on these platforms, making them proficient and current. Use a good-quality profile picture, making it interesting and even more compelling by including descriptions where relevant to ease other users' accessibility.

Be Consistent Across Platforms: Good use of various platforms ensures consistency in terms of brand image. Also, use the same profile photo, username, and other brand personality to grow yourself so that it is easy for people to recognize you.

Engage Actively: Find relevant content to share regularly, follow up with comments on posts, and engage in discussions. Being active demonstrates that you take a keen interest in developing personal relationships and making the best use of their implications.

Join Groups and Communities: It is a home for several places offering groups or communities where kindred individuals can team up. Visit societies or groups within your chosen field of interest and network with professionals with the same interests.

Start Your Groups or Events: You might be interested in forming your groups, webinars, or events that you can hold on a topic about which you are well informed. You can become a thought leader and wildlife connections knocking at your door, yearning for knowledge.

Personalize Connection Requests: When greeting fellow users for a connection, give a friendly message. State below why you would like to establish a link or how this connection may benefit from the collaboration. Generically worded questions are only sometimes practical.

Share Valuable Content: Be generous in sharing wholesome content on your profiles. For example, you can repost articles in your field on topics relating to social phenomena or videos, graphics, and statistics—anything relevant—as well as share personal insights. By regularly publishing engaging content with patience and persistence, you increase your visibility and reputation.

Are you interested in finding, at least, potential clients or mentees and between mentors working conditions partnership opportunities? If you have set clear goals for yourself, your actions will always be consistent. For this:

Maintain Privacy: Remember to select social media privacy settings and what you publish online. Cover sensitive information and show that your online life well presents you as the persona of an aspiring specialist.

Use Advanced Search Features: As with most platforms, these platforms offer features that perform in-depth searches involving various elements, such as professionals and organizations. These features help you find and reach out to people with similar intentions.

Follow-Up and Nurture Relationships: Strengthening relationships is the real deal! People are more likely to invest in your project if they get help from you, so periodically, I recommend that the team keep nurturing relationships by setting up follow-up calls with their connections and helping them out because only when people feel personally obligated will invest in someone else's projects make sense for businesspeople.

Be Authentic and Respectful. Authentic and respectful informal relationships formed entirely in cyberspace are long-lasting. Respect colleagues by being helpful and friendly but maintaining a business-like approach. Do not be spammy or unnecessarily promotional.

Measure and Adapt: Track your networking and collaboration efforts to find out what works. If results are unsatisfactory or your connections do not react as you prefer, change something and try to adjust.

Remember that establishing meaningful online relationships requires time and consistency, so be patient and keep trying. Whether you are an entrepreneur, a professional, or even any organization itself, online platforms can be handy tools that will help you grow your network and get new people around you in touch with whom everyone can achieve their objectives.

Conclusion

Challenges and opportunities lie ahead in a world of constant change and evolving work environments. This chapter offers ideas for individuals and organizations to thrive in this dynamic future.

Career agility starts with self-assessment and a commitment to lifelong learning. Personal development plans help individuals adapt, adjust, and discover new opportunities.

Organizations also need to embrace adaptability and resilience to survive and excel. By promoting leadership approaches that foster these qualities, organizations can navigate uncertainties and thrive in changing circumstances.

Collaboration is crucial for progress, especially in the digital age, where connections are made through online platforms. Learning to collaborate and utilize digital tools helps build networks and capture new knowledge efficiently.

Embracing change is essential for success in a rapidly changing world. Instead of fearing change, we should see it as an opportunity for growth and maturity, prompting us to adopt new experiences. The tactics outlined in this chapter—adaptability, resilience, collaboration, and learning—serve as a roadmap for confidently navigating the challenges and opportunities of the future.

Success in this dynamic world is about reaching endpoints and navigating change nimbly. By being adaptable, setting compelling goals, and fostering creative interactions, individuals and organizations can embark on this journey confidently, ready to capitalize on opportunities.

Conclusion

In synthesizing the diverse landscape of the evolving world of work, we must acknowledge our current state as rooted in the seeds sown by our past. This future, while volatile, is brimming with promise, propelled forward by technological innovation, societal dynamics, and the aspirations of those shaping its trajectory today. Across the chapters of this comprehensive exploration, various facets of this complex terrain have been revealed, offering readers diverse perspectives and pathways forward.

From the advent of automation during the Industrial Revolution to the present era of artificial intelligence and remote operations, we have witnessed the emergence of new industries and a shift from rigid industrial structures to more flexible, scalable, and individual-focused technologies that prioritize creativity. This transformative journey underscores the pivotal role of education as a guiding light, empowering humanity to transition from the shadows of monotony into the brilliance of innovation and progress.

In this environment, interruption is presented as an opportunity instead of a threat for proactive innovators. These individuals are willing to embrace change and allow innovative culture to take shape within them. With the revolutionary boost of technology, the human factor will always be crucial—the mental health, relations between people, and the workforce, which is cared for and appreciated, is a priority.

Organizations in the contemporary age must be proactive in embracing and accommodating diversity ethically and from a business standpoint. Government policies ensure fair labor distribution and protect workers from market forces.

As we move forward, personal adaptability, resilience-building, and collaboration are desirable and essential qualities for success in navigating the evolving landscape. By fostering these qualities, businesses can equip their workforce to seize opportunities and drive change and innovation.

While the future holds promise, it is also marked by uncertainty. However, within this uncertainty lies opportunities for transformative change. Embracing optimism and embracing change are essential to unlocking growth, innovation, and progress, utilizing the strategies outlined in these chapters.

The concept of success is redefined to focus not only on reaching a destination but also on navigating through an ever-changing environment. The future workplace is depicted as a dynamic landscape where adaptability, resilience, and collaboration are tools for creative expression. Learning is embraced as a lifelong journey, with each professional endeavor contributing to one's overall lifestyle and personal growth.

As individuals and organizations navigate our world's transformative journey, it's essential to discern the paths they choose for themselves. Those prepared to seize the opportunities presented by a rapidly evolving future will view survival not merely as a possibility but as a potential for prosperity. In this dynamic landscape of constant change, success will not be a distant prospect but a tangible reality to strive for.

References

An Insight into BMW Supply Chain Strategy: A Perfect Guide - 2023. (2023, August 6). https://dfreight.org/blog/an-insight-into-bmw-supply-chain-strategy/#:~:text=The%20company%20leverages%20technologies%20like

Armstrong, P. (2023). *Disruptive Technologies.* Kogan Page Publishers.

BBC. (2018, January 23). Netflix's history: From DVD rentals to streaming success. *BBC News.* https://www.bbc.com/news/newsbeat-42788099

Chan, L., Hogaboam, L., & Cao, R. (2022). *Applied artificial intelligence in business : concepts and cases.* Springer.

Day, M. (2016, December 12). *How Microsoft emerged from the darkness to embrace the cloud.* The Seattle Times. https://www.seattletimes.com/business/technology/how-microsoft-emerged-from-darkness-to-embrace-the-cloud/

Edghiem, F., Ali, M., & Wood, R. (2023). *Digital Entrepreneurship and Co-Creating Value Through Digital Encounters.* IGI Global.

Even, A. M., & Christiansen, B. (2023). *Enhancing Employee Engagement and Productivity in the Post-Pandemic Multigenerational Workforce.* IGI Global.

Georghiou, A. (n.d.). *Uncovering Unconscious Bias in Recruiting and Interviewing.* Knoxville Happiness Coalition.

Gibbons, P. (2015). *The science of successful organizational change : how leaders set strategy, change behavior, and create an Agile culture.* Pearson Education.

Greengard, S. (2015). *The internet of things.* Mit Press.

Haan, K. (2023, June 12). Remote Work Statistics And Trends In 2023. *Forbes*. https://www.forbes.com/advisor/business/remote-work-statistics/

Hardesty, L. (2018, February 11). *Study finds gender and skin-type bias in commercial artificial-intelligence systems*. MIT News; Massachusetts Institute of Technology. https://news.mit.edu/2018/study-finds-gender-skin-type-bias-artificial-intelligence-systems-0212

Herrmann, A., Brenner, W., & Stadler, R. (2018). *Autonomous driving : how the driverless revolution will change the world*. Emerald Publishing.

Kelso, A. (n.d.). *How Becoming "A Tech Company That Sells Pizza" Delivered Huge For Domino's*. Forbes. Retrieved February 2, 2024, from https://www.forbes.com/sites/aliciakelso/2018/04/30/delivery-digital-provide-dominos-with-game-changing-advantages/?sh=4c80187b7771

Marr, B. (2022). *Future Skills The 20 Skills and Competencies Everyone Needs to Succeed in a Digital World*. John Wiley & Sons, Incorporated.

Mckinnon, P. (2015). *Robotics : everything you need to know about robotics from beginner to expert*. Peter Mckinnon.

Moorman, C. (n.d.). *Adobe: How To Dominate The Subscription Economy*. Forbes. Retrieved February 2, 2024, from https://www.forbes.com/sites/christinemoorman/2018/08/23/adobe-how-to-dominate-the-subscription-economy/?sh=6adda23352e8

Mulcahy, D. (2017). *The gig economy : the complete guide to getting better work, taking more time off, and financing the life you want*. Amacom, American Management Assoication.

Noble, D. (2017). *FORCES OF PRODUCTION : a social history of industrial automation*.

Sacolick, I. (2017). *Driving digital : the leader's guide to business transformation through technology*. Amacom, American Management Association.

Sava, J. A. (2020, July 3). *Remote work frequency before/after COVID-19 2020*. Statista. https://www.statista.com/statistics/1122987/change-in-remote-work-trends-after-covid-in-usa/

Schramm, E., Lahmann, C., Allwang, C., Kahl, K. G., & Lang, U. E. (2021). *Promoting Mental Health at Work: New Insights and Practical Implications*. Frontiers Media SA.

The Future of Lifelong Learning and Work. (2008). BRILL.

Valerio De Stefano, Durri, I., Charalampos Stylogiannis, & Wouters, M. (2022). *A Research Agenda for the Gig Economy and Society*. Edward Elgar Publishing.

Verdegem, P. (2021). *AI for Everyone?* University of Westminster Press.

Warren, C. R. (2022). *How to Be a Diversity and Inclusion Ambassador*. Berrett-Koehler Publishers.

Watt, M., & Australia. Parliament. Senate. Select Committee On The Future Of Work And Workers. (2018). *Hope is not a strategy - our shared responsibility for the future of work and workers*. Select Committee On The Future Of Work And Workers.

Webber, M., Sarris, A., & Bessell, M. (2010). Organisational Culture and the Use of Work–Life Balance Initiatives: Influence on Work Attitudes and Work–Life Conflict. *The Australian and New Zealand Journal of Organisational Psychology*, *3*, 54–65. https://doi.org/10.1375/ajop.3.1.54

Whiteman, R. (2023). *Artificially Human*. Better Future Publishing.

Zykova, N. M., & Maussymbek, Sh. T. (2021). Analysis of advantages and disadvantages of remote work. *Bulletin Series Psychology*, *66*(1), 40–45. https://doi.org/10.51889/2021-1.1728-7847.07

www.ingramcontent.com/pod-product-compliance
Lightning Source LLC
LaVergne TN
LVHW051239050326
832903LV00028B/2464
9798328983228